T0143001

An Analysis of

Alan D. Baddeley and Graham Hitch's

Working Memory

Birgit Koopmann-Holm
with
Alexander J. O'Connor

Published by Macat International Ltd
24:13 Coda Centre, 189 Munster Road, London SW6 6AW.

Distributed exclusively by Routledge
2 Park Square, Milton Park, Abingdon, Oxon OX14 4RN
711 Third Avenue, New York, NY 10017, USA

Routledge is an imprint of the Taylor & Francis Group, an informa business

www.macat.com
info@macat.com

Cataloguing in Publication Data
A catalogue record for this book is available from the British Library.
Library of Congress Cataloguing-in-Publication Data is available upon request.
Cover illustration: Etienne Gilfillan

ISBN 978-1-912303-53-3 (hardback)
ISBN 978-1-912128-72-3 (paperback)
ISBN 978-1-912282-41-8 (e-book)

Notice
The information in this book is designed to orientate readers of the work under analysis,
to elucidate and contextualise its key ideas and themes, and to aid in the development
of critical thinking skills. It is not meant to be used, nor should it be used, as a
substitute for original thinking or in place of original writing or research. References and
notes are provided for informational purposes and their presence does not constitute
endorsement of the information or opinions therein. This book is presented solely for
educational purposes. It is sold on the understanding that the publisher is not engaged
to provide any scholarly advice. The publisher has made every effort to ensure that
this book is accurate and up-to-date, but makes no warranties or representations with
regard to the completeness or reliability of the information it contains. The information
and the opinions provided herein are not guaranteed or warranted to produce particular
results and may not be suitable for students of every ability. The publisher shall not be
liable for any loss, damage or disruption arising from any errors or omissions, or from
the use of this book, including, but not limited to, special, incidental, consequential or
other damages caused, or alleged to have been caused, directly or indirectly, by the
information contained within.

CONTENTS

THE MACAT LIBRARY

The Macat Library is a series of unique academic explorations of seminal works in the humanities and social sciences – books and papers that have had a significant and widely recognised impact on their disciplines. It has been created to serve as much more than just a summary of what lies between the covers of a great book. It illuminates and explores the influences on, ideas of, and impact of that book. Our goal is to offer a learning resource that encourages critical thinking and fosters a better, deeper understanding of important ideas.

Each publication is divided into three Sections: Influences, Ideas, and Impact. Each Section has four Modules. These explore every important facet of the work, and the responses to it.

This Section-Module structure makes a Macat Library book easy to use, but it has another important feature. Because each Macat book is written to the same format, it is possible (and encouraged!) to cross-reference multiple Macat books along the same lines of inquiry or research. This allows the reader to open up interesting interdisciplinary pathways.

To further aid your reading, lists of glossary terms and people mentioned are included at the end of this book (these are indicated by an asterisk [*] throughout) – as well as a list of works cited.

Macat has worked with the University of Cambridge to identify the elements of critical thinking and understand the ways in which six different skills combine to enable effective thinking.
Three allow us to fully understand a problem; three more give us the tools to solve it. Together, these six skills make up the **PACIER** model of critical thinking. They are:

ANALYSIS – understanding how an argument is built
EVALUATION – exploring the strengths and weaknesses of an argument
INTERPRETATION – understanding issues of meaning

CREATIVE THINKING – coming up with new ideas and fresh connections
PROBLEM-SOLVING – producing strong solutions
REASONING – creating strong arguments

To find out more, visit **WWW.MACAT.COM.**

CRITICAL THINKING AND "WORKING MEMORY"

Primary critical thinking skill: PROBLEM-SOLVING
Secondary critical thinking skill: EVALUTION

The work of memory researchers Alan Baddeley and Graham Hitch is a prime example of the ways in which good critical thinkers approach questions and the problems they raise.

In the 1960s, researchers into human memory began to understand memory as comprising not one, but two systems. The first was a short-term system handling information for mere seconds. The second was a long-term system capable of managing information indefinitely. They also discovered, however, that short-term memory was not simply a 'filing cabinet,' as many had thought, but was actively working on cognitive – or mental – tasks. This is how the phrase "working memory" developed. The hypothesis remained unproven, however, presenting Baddeley and Hitch with the problem of working out how to produce definitive evidence that short-term memory was a working system that actively manipulated and processed information.

They responded by designing a series of ten experiments aimed at showing just this – presenting the results in their 1974 article, 'Working Memory.' The research was a masterpiece of problem-solving that proved revelatory. The authors not only generated new solutions and made sound decisions between alternative possibilities – they also showed that short-term memory is indeed an active system responsible for information processing and managing, while also influencing attention, reasoning, reading comprehension and learning.

While their work has since been refined by others, Baddeley and Hitch's problem-solving approach helped to create the dominant understanding of working memory that underpins psychological research throughout the world today.

ABOUT THE AUTHORS OF THE ORIGINAL WORK

Alan Baddeley is a cognitive psychologist best known for his research on human memory. He is currently professor of psychology at the University of York. His 1974 paper 'Working Memory,' which he wrote in collaboration with **Graham Hitch**, and the additions he has since made to the original work, have established him as the world's leading expert on short-term memory. Baddeley's work is now considered an excellent entry point into the whole field of human memory, and the Baddeley–Hitch model remains dominant in the field. Baddeley remains a prolific researcher, with over 600 publications and 11 books to his name.

ABOUT THE AUTHORS OF THE ANALYSIS

Dr Birgit Koopmann–Holm holds a doctorate in psychology from Stanford University. She currently teaches in the Department of Psychology at Santa Clara University, California.

Dr Alexander O'Connor did his postgraduate work at the University of California, Berkeley, where he received a PhD for work on social and personality psychology.

ABOUT MACAT

GREAT WORKS FOR CRITICAL THINKING

Macat is focused on making the ideas of the world's great thinkers accessible and comprehensible to everybody, everywhere, in ways that promote the development of enhanced critical thinking skills.

It works with leading academics from the world's top universities to produce new analyses that focus on the ideas and the impact of the most influential works ever written across a wide variety of academic disciplines. Each of the works that sit at the heart of its growing library is an enduring example of great thinking. But by setting them in context – and looking at the influences that shaped their authors, as well as the responses they provoked – Macat encourages readers to look at these classics and game-changers with fresh eyes. Readers learn to think, engage and challenge their ideas, rather than simply accepting them.

'Macat offers an amazing first-of-its-kind tool for interdisciplinary learning and research. Its focus on works that transformed their disciplines and its rigorous approach, drawing on the world's leading experts and educational institutions, opens up a world-class education to anyone.'

Andreas Schleicher,
Director for Education and Skills, Organisation for Economic
Co-operation and Development

'Macat is taking on some of the major challenges in university education ... They have drawn together a strong team of active academics who are producing teaching materials that are novel in the breadth of their approach.'

Prof Lord Broers,
former Vice-Chancellor of the University of Cambridge

'The Macat vision is exceptionally exciting. It focuses upon new modes of learning which analyse and explain seminal texts which have profoundly influenced world thinking and so social and economic development. It promotes the kind of critical thinking which is essential for any society and economy. This is the learning of the future.'

Rt Hon Charles Clarke, former UK Secretary of State for Education

'The Macat analyses provide immediate access to the critical conversation surrounding the books that have shaped their respective discipline, which will make them an invaluable resource to all of those, students and teachers, working in the field.'

Professor William Tronzo, University of California at San Diego

WAYS IN TO THE TEXT

KEY POINTS

- The English cognitive psychologist* Alan D. Baddeley was born in 1934 and began his academic career working with leaders in the field of memory* research.

- In "Working Memory," published in 1974, Baddeley and co-author Graham Hitch proposed a new way—or model—to describe short-term memory.*

- This model remains the most used framework for understanding short-term memory.

Who Is Alan D. Baddeley?

Born in England in 1934, Alan D. Baddeley is a cognitive psychologist best known for his research on human memory. Cognitive psychology is an area of psychology that examines basic mental processes such as memory, language, attention, and perception.

Baddeley received his PhD at the University of Cambridge in 1962, where his career as a memory researcher began. While at Cambridge, he worked at the Medical Research Council Applied Psychology Unit (APU) developing postal codes that could be remembered easily. R. Conrad* and Donald Broadbent,* two leading memory researchers who became inspirations and mentors to Baddeley, advised him at the APU.

In 1971, Baddeley accepted Graham Hitch as his postdoctoral fellow.* A year later, they both moved to the University of Stirling in Scotland, where they wrote the paper, "Working Memory." Published in 1974, it established Baddeley as a leading memory researcher. Over the following decades, he became the world's leading expert on short-term memory.

Two developments in the 1950s and 1960s were particularly relevant to the understanding of short-term/working memory that Baddeley and Hitch created. The first was the advent of the computer, which memory researchers such as Donald Broadbent began using as an analogy to explain the inner workings of the human mind. The second was the shift in psychology away from behaviorism,* which had avoided the study of memory. Behaviorists tended to view cognitive factors—such as thinking—as less relevant than the actions people actually took and recommended studying observable behaviors.

What became known as the cognitive revolution* began in the 1950s in several fields, such as psychology, anthropology, and linguistics. This movement focused on studying the internal thoughts, attitudes, motivations, and values that people use to make sense of the world and interact with it. As the cognitive revolution became less reliant on behaviorism, memory and the study of cognition*—all the mental abilities and processes associated with knowledge—became central research topics.

What Does "Working Memory" Say?

In the 1960s, memory researchers such as Richard C. Atkinson* and Richard M. Shiffrin* began to view memory as two systems: 1) a short-term system capable of handling information for just seconds and 2) a long-term* system that could theoretically store and manage information indefinitely. Many researchers, including Atkinson and Shiffrin, argued that the short-term system was active, not passive. In other words, short-term memory was thought to be *working*—actually involved in cognitive tasks—rather just being a passive store* of information. Indeed, by the early 1970s, researchers increasingly termed short-term memory a working memory* system.

These two concepts—first, the distinction between short-term and long-term memory and, second, short-term memory as working memory—became accepted beliefs for memory researchers. But questions arose about how the systems were structured and functioned. The Atkinson–Shiffrin model* assumed that short-term/working memory was a single component that handled, stored, and manipulated all types of information. New research suggested, however, that a system with specialized functions might better describe short-term memory.

Baddeley and Hitch were looking for experimental evidence that would shed light on the structure of short-term memory and prove that it could be described as a working memory system. "Working Memory" provides details of that proof. In it, Baddeley and Hitch present the results of 10 original experiments and conclude that working memory consists of three components. They argue that two separate components—one handling verbal/acoustic information (what we hear) and the other handling visual and spatial information (what we see)—control short-term information storage. They later referred to the verbal/acoustic component as "the phonological loop"* and the visual/spatial component as "the visuo-spatial sketchpad."* Baddeley and Hitch called the third component the central executive.* This is responsible for processing and managing the two storage components, as well as influencing attention, reasoning, reading comprehension, and learning.

Baddeley and Hitch demonstrated this theory through several experiments. For instance, they had participants recite a series of numbers, which requires use of the phonological loop to rehearse and temporarily store those numbers. At the same time, they asked the participants to complete a reasoning task, such as deciding whether a series of sentences was grammatical. Baddeley and Hitch argued that since the phonological loop was already occupied, this task needed another component: the central executive. So they developed a multi-component working memory system—one that is still dominant today. The Baddeley–Hitch model* has been modified in recent decades, but continues to inspire researchers—some looking for confirmation of the model, others looking to apply the model to other fields.

Why Does "Working Memory" Matter?

"Working Memory" provides the origins and framework of the dominant model for understanding short-term memory. The Baddeley–Hitch model, as it is known, is termed a working memory model. It presents a view that short-term memory is more than just a filing cabinet of information: it is actively involved in reasoning, reading comprehension, and learning. Later work finds it also involved with other areas of cognition.*

"Working Memory" is also a highly effective entry point to studying human memory. It not only contains a concise overview of the research and models developed in the 1960s and early 1970s, but it also details the issues with some of these earlier models that originally led to the Baddeley–Hitch model. The text can introduce readers to some of the more common experimental designs and methods used in cognitive psychology.

In the dual-task paradigm,* for instance, participants perform two tasks simultaneously. This allows researchers to examine the relationship between proposed brain functions and performance. Baddeley and Hitch asked participants to recite a series of words or numbers while also performing a reasoning task. Performance was generally similar even when participants completed the tasks simultaneously or separately, suggesting that the two tasks rely on different brain structures. The dual-task paradigm is still a valuable technique in experimental psychology.

Memory plays an integral role in everyday life and, as a result, the Baddeley–Hitch model has been applied to many other fields outside of cognitive psychology. One such area is developmental psychology,* where research examines memory capabilities across the human lifespan. Medical researchers have also used the model, for instance, as a framework for understanding and predicting diseases associated with memory loss, such as Alzheimer's.*

Today neuroimaging* methods that allow researchers to view the structure and function of the brain are providing a new avenue for research on the Baddeley–Hitch model. The model is as relevant as ever, and "Working Memory" is a key text, serving as an entry point to the study of human memory.

SECTION 1
INFLUENCES

MODULE 1
THE AUTHOR AND THE HISTORICAL CONTEXT

KEY POINTS

- "Working Memory" provides the foundation for our understanding of the structure and function of short-term memory.

- Baddeley's research, funded by the United Kingdom Post Office, was the beginning of his study of memory.

- The advent and growth of computing in the 1950s through the 1970s helped Baddeley and Hitch understand human memory.

Why Read This Text?

"Working Memory" is an influential 1974 paper in which Alan D. Baddeley and Graham Hitch described the original version of their short-term memory* model, a system they call working memory.* The term reflects their belief that the short-term memory system is not just a passive store,* accumulating information like a filing drawer. On the contrary, memory plays an active role and is *working* when we reason, comprehend, and learn new information.

Baddeley and Hitch also proposed a working memory system that has multiple parts, or components. These components include two units for the storage of information—one for visual information and one for verbal information. In addition, Baddeley and Hitch described a third unit that processes this information. This model, consisting of three components, contradicted the belief at the time that a single unit controlled all these processes. Their multicomponent view of short-

> ❝ On return [from conducting research in the US], I didn't have a PhD place, and the only job I could get was as a hospital porter and later as a secondary modern school teacher—with no training whatsoever! Then a job cropped up at the Medical Research Council Applied Psychology Unit in Cambridge. They had a project funded by the Post Office on the design of postal codes and so I started doing research on memory. ❞
>
> Alan D. Baddeley, interview in *The Psychologist*

term memory remains the dominant model of human memory. Furthermore, Baddeley and Hitch were the first researchers to show *through experiment* that working memory is key to reading, comprehending, reasoning, and learning.

Since the original publication of "Working Memory," various scholars have made modifications and additions to the Baddeley–Hitch model.* The text and model, however, are still highly influential in memory research. "Working Memory" has been cited more than 10,000 times. In 1992, Baddeley presented a summary of research that had taken place since the original publication. That paper has itself been cited over 17,000 times since.[1] In 2000, Baddeley updated the original model, adding a fourth component in a paper that has been cited over 5,000 times.[2]

Author's Life

Alan D. Baddeley was born in England in 1934. His father was a compositor* in Hunslet, a working-class district of Leeds in Yorkshire, England. Baddeley graduated with a BA in psychology from University College London in 1956. A year later, he received his MA from Princeton University.

He then moved to the Medical Research Council Applied Psychology Unit (APU) at the University of Cambridge, where he worked on the development of easily remembered postal codes. This earned him his PhD in 1962.[3] Baddeley's time at the APU marked his start as a memory researcher. His mentor at the APU was applied psychologist R. Conrad,* who was instrumental in developing some of the concepts Baddeley would later integrate into his working memory model.[4]

Baddeley continued at the APU until 1967, when he accepted a teaching post at the University of Sussex. In 1971, he employed Graham Hitch, a postdoctoral fellow,* to study the relationships between short- and long-term memory.* A year later, both moved to the University of Stirling in Scotland, where they wrote "Working Memory."[5]

Author's Background

From early in his career, Baddeley was interested in using psychology to address issues in the real world. "I entered psychology as a student at University College London in 1953, a very exciting time for the field of psychology, which had benefited greatly from developments during World War II,* where theory was enriched by the need to tackle practical problems."[6]

The arrival of computers in this postwar period influenced many academics, and this was true of Baddeley, Hitch, and other cognitive psychologists.* For memory researchers, the advent of computer science* suggested comparisons and analogies between the workings of a computer and the workings of the human mind and memory.

Baddeley was exposed to this approach of applying computer science and computational thinking while at the APU. He remembered that, during this time, the APU's director, Donald Broadbent,* "had just published his key book *Perception and Communication*, showing how theoretical models, influenced by the newly developing area of computer science, could provide tools for investigating attention, perception, and memory, problems that had been regarded as difficult to address by earlier behaviorist* approaches."[7] Baddeley and Hitch saw similarities between the computer and human memory, hence their use of computer terminology (for example, "memory store," "central processor," and the like) to describe their components of working memory.

NOTES

1 Alan Baddeley, "Working Memory," Science 255, no. 5044 (1992): 556–9.

2 Alan Baddeley, "The Episodic Buffer: A New Component of Working Memory?," *Trends in Cognitive Sciences* 4, no. 11 (2000): 417.

3 A. D. Baddeley, "Awards for Distinguished Scientific Contributions Is Working Memory Still Working?," *American Psychologist* 56, no. 11 (2001): 849.

4 John Groeger, "The Working Memory Man," *The Psychologist*, 7, no. 2 (1994): 58.

5 Baddeley, "Awards," 850.

6 Alan Baddeley, "Working Memory: Theories, Models, and Controversies," *Annual Review of Psychology* 63 (2012): 3.

7 Baddeley, "Awards," 850.

MODULE 2
ACADEMIC CONTEXT

KEY POINTS

- The cognitive revolution* placed greater emphasis on understanding the inner workings of the mind.

- In the 1960s, the cognitive revolution and the development of computer science* led to human memory models that were based on the way computers worked.

- Donald Broadbent,* a pioneer of both the cognitive revolution and applying computer models as an analogy for human memory, mentored Baddeley.

The Work in its Context

By the 1970s, psychology was in the middle of a fundamental change of thinking that is often labeled the cognitive revolution. Researchers began to focus on cognitive* factors— the mental abilities and processes associated with knowledge, such as attitudes, beliefs, and memory* processing—to predict and explain behavior. Prior to that time, a framework called behaviorism,* which suggested that most human behavior was the result of conditioned responses,* dominated psychology.

Conditioned response refers to an integral mechanism through which, behaviorists argue, learning occurs. It is a behavior that is learned through association with other events. For example, the behaviorist might say that we don't touch a hot stove because in early life we have experienced that touching hot things leads to pain and burns. The reinforcement,* in this example, is the burn—it reinforces our behavior by associating *hot* with *pain*. Behaviorism suggests that cognitive states such as thinking were not a factor in predicting and

> ❝ Neither side was able to deliver a knockout blow, and people simply abandoned the research area. ❞
>
> Alan D. Baddeley, quoted in *The Psychologist* on the debate over behaviorism in the 1960s

explaining human behavior.

Behaviorism is concerned only with observable behavior. It ignores internal, mental states such as memory. Many behaviorists believe that direct observation of behavior is the only scientific method for understanding human psychology.

Alan D. Baddeley began his career as a behaviorist, but quickly moved on as he witnessed the decline in the popularity of behaviorism. He later wrote, "When I graduated [from college] I went to the States for a year hoping, when I returned [to the UK], to do research on partial reinforcement in rats. But when I came back the whole behaviourist enterprise was largely in ruins. The big controversy … had apparently been abandoned as a draw, and everybody moved on to do something else."[1] As the cognitive revolution replaced behaviorism in the 1960s, the study of internal mental workings like memory grew rapidly, leading to Baddeley and Hitch's work.

Overview of the Field

Within cognitive psychology,* and more specifically memory research, researchers in the 1960s began using computer analogies and adapting computing theories to understand and explain human memory. These adaptations suggest that components of human memory are like the components of a computer.

For instance, just as a computer has a central processor responsible for actively manipulating information, researchers began to assume a similar processor existed in human minds. Donald Broadbent,* in his 1958 text *Perception and Communication*, suggests that we can understand the human mind by applying knowledge about how computers work.

Information theory* was key to both the cognitive revolution and the application of computing principles to understanding the mind. This theory provides a framework for measuring how information or data is transmitted between devices, components, and so on. One of its most important principles, both for computing and in developing theories of human memory, is that information flow is limited.[2] When information theory is applied to psychology, people can be seen as information processors with limited capacity—meaning that a mind can process or work with only so much information at any one time.

Before Baddeley and Graham Hitch wrote "Working Memory" in 1974, several models describing short-term memory* existed. Most said that memory has a limited capacity. The most prominent model is the Atkinson–Shiffrin Model,*[3] named after its founders, Richard C. Atkinson* and Richard M. Shiffrin.* This model suggests that one short-term store* also functions as working memory.* In other words, a single construct stores all new information as it makes its way into memory.

Academic Influences

Baddeley's mentor at the APU in Cambridge was R. Conrad,* an applied psychologist interested in short-term memory. Conrad is best known for his work on the acoustic similarity effect:* a phenomenon whereby a list of letters that sound similar (such as *b, g, e*) is more difficult to remember than a list of letters that sound different (such as *k, r, y*). Baddeley worked with Conrad on developing UK postal codes that would be remembered easily.

In fact, in "Working Memory," Baddeley and Hitch examine the effects of acoustic similarity in one of their studies. Another of Baddeley's inspirations was APU director Donald Broadbent.* Baddeley would later remark that Broadbent's influential text *Perception* *and Communication* was "the seminal book on the cognitive revolution."[4]

Philosophers, particularly philosophers of science like Karl Popper* and Imre Lakatos,* also influenced Baddeley. He wrote that, during his time at the University of Cambridge, his own ideas on the purpose of research changed to be more in line with the later writings of Lakatos and Popper. Baddeley came to believe "that the mark of a good theory is that it should be productive, not only giving an account of existing knowledge, but also generating fruitful questions that will increase our knowledge."[5] Indeed, "Working Memory" became so influential in part because it asked fruitful questions that Baddeley and Hitch did not, at the time, have answers for.

NOTES

1   "Interview with Alan Baddeley," *The Psychologist*, accessed June 5, 2015, https://thepsychologist.bps.org.uk/volume-24/edition-5/interview-alan-baddeley

2   Claude Elwood Shannon, "A Mathematical Theory of Communication," *ACM SIGMOBILE Mobile Computing and Communications Review* 5, no. 1 (2001): 3–55.

3   Richard C. Atkinson and Richard M. Shiffrin, "Human Memory: A Proposed System and Its Control Processes," *The Psychology of Learning and Motivation: Advances in Research and Theory*, vol. 2, ed. Kenneth W. Spence and Janet T. Spence (New York: Academic Press, 1968), 89–195.

4   Ian Baddeley, "Alan Baddeley on the Cognitive Revolution," YouTube video, 5:10, posted by "gocognitive," October 27, 2010, https://www.youtube.com/watch?v=wyfEETtWgCY

5   Alan Baddeley, "Working Memory: Theories, Models, and Controversies," *Annual Review of Psychology* 63 (2012): 4.

THE PROBLEM

KEY POINTS

- Several theoretical models of short-term memory* existed before Alan D. Baddeley and Graham Hitch wrote "Working Memory," but, without much actual evidence behind them, the validity of those models was in question.
- The Atkinson–Shiffrin short-term memory model* suggests a single component to short-term memory that is responsible for storage, processing, and transfer to long-term memory.
- Baddeley and Hitch incorporated findings that called into question the Atkinson–Shiffrin model and allowed these findings to guide their work in "Working Memory."

Core Question

In writing "Working Memory," Alan D. Baddeley and Graham Hitch wanted to provide evidence for the structure and function of short-term memory.* At the time, researchers generally agreed that separate short-term and long-term memory* systems existed: the former handled temporary information (like this sentence) and the latter handled longer-term information (like your birthday). The focus in "Working Memory" was on the short-term system.

In the introduction to the paper, Baddeley and Hitch write, "Despite more than a decade of intensive research on the topic of short-term memory, we still know virtually nothing about its role in normal human information processing."[1] Other researchers had used the term working memory* in the decade before Baddeley and Hitch published their paper. By labeling this short-term memory system as *working*, they indicated that the system was *actively* involved in

> 66 By the end of the 1960s ... problems with the modal [dominant] model were starting to emerge. 99
>
> Alan D. Baddeley, quoted in *The Psychologist* on the debate over the Atkinson–Shiffrin model

processing information. In other words, it was not just a store* of information, but was actually involved in *doing* something with that information—such as helping with learning, decision-making, etc. But again, there was little observed evidence that this was the case.

Baddeley and Hitch wanted to answer two core questions through experiment. First, they were looking for evidence that would detail the *structure* of short-term memory. Second, they wanted to test the assumption that working memory played a function in performance tasks such as comprehending, reasoning, and learning.

The Participants

The prominent short-term memory model prior to the Baddeley and Hitch paper was one that Richard C. Atkinson* and Richard M. Shiffrin* had developed. This model proposes a single short-term store that also acts as working memory. Stores refer to structures or components of the brain that actually hold information and memories. Both short- and long-term memory have stores. Further, within the working memory model, each component is capable of storage.

Baddeley later described the Atkinson–Shiffrin model as follows: "One model, however, became dominant, so much so as to be named the 'modal model.' This model was proposed by Atkinson and Shiffrin (1968), who also claimed it to be a working memory model which, in addition to providing short-term storage, was capable of such complex activities as selecting strategies, controlling input to LTM [long-term memory], guiding retrieval and much else."[2]

For example, if you were trying to remember a street address, the

Atkinson–Shiffrin model proposes that a single component, which they called working memory, holds this address and sends it into long-term memory. The Atkinson–Shiffrin model also proposes that information in short-term memory is transferred to long-term memory primarily as a function of time—that is, the longer something is held in short-term memory, the more likely it is that it will move over to long-term memory. Baddeley believed there was little observed evidence for this theory. He later recalled, "The assumption that material held in the short-term store would automatically transfer to LTM, with duration in store linked to amount learned, proved unjustified."[3]

The Contemporary Debate

In the years before the publication of Baddeley and Hitch's paper, other memory researchers began questioning the Atkinson–Shiffrin model. There is no clear evidence, however, that Atkinson or Shiffrin engaged in a debate with any of these researchers. In fact, Baddeley suggests that, by the early 1970s, even though there was considerable questioning of the Atkinson–Shiffrin model, few researchers were interested in developing another model.

Baddeley recalls the attitude in the early 1970s: "At this point many investigators into STM [short-term memory] moved on to other more recently developing areas."[4] The Atkinson–Shiffrin model is broader than most memory models in that it attempts to describe the entire memory process—from the perception of new information, to its placement in short-term/working memory, then its transfer to long-term memory. Baddeley and Hitch were more focused on exploring the structure and function of the short-term model. Further, in their seminal 1968 text, Atkinson and Shiffrin themselves note the evolving nature of their incomplete theory, just as Baddeley and Hitch would in "Working Memory." Atkinson and Shiffrin wrote: "These first sections of the paper do not present a finished theory; instead they set forth a general framework within which specific models can be formulated."[5]

But results from several areas of psychology began to question the short-term/working memory component of the Atkinson–Shiffrin model. Most notable was the research that Fergus I. M. Craik* and Robert S. Lockhart* published in 1972. The Atkinson–Shiffrin model argues that holding and rehearsing information in short-term memory is the best, and possibly only, way to learn. But Craik and Lockhart found that the more *deeply* people process and engage with information—such as using strategies to make it more meaningful and memorable—the more likely they are to learn it. For instance, people are more likely to remember the sequence of letters *Y, R, O, M, E, M* when they realize the letters are the reverse of the word *MEMORY* than if they simply try to memorize the original sequence.

NOTES

1   Alan D. Baddeley and Graham Hitch, "Working Memory," *Psychology of Learning and Motivation* 8 (1974): 47–48.

2   "Looking Back: How It All Began," *The Psychologist,* accessed June 5, 2015, https://thepsychologist.bps.org.uk/volume-28/april-2015/looking-back-how-it-all-began.

3   "Looking Back," *The Psychologist.*

4   "Looking Back," *The Psychologist.*

5   Richard C. Atkinson and Richard M. Shiffrin, "Human Memory: A Proposed System and Its Control Processes," *The Psychology of Learning and Motivation: Advances in Research and Theory*, vol. 2, ed. Kenneth W. Spence and Janet T. Spence (New York: Academic Press, 1968): 92.

MODULE 4
THE AUTHOR'S CONTRIBUTION

KEY POINTS

- Baddeley and Hitch looked for evidence that clarified the structure and function of the short-term memory* system.

- In doing so, they found support for a working memory* system made up of separate components.

- Earlier research had oversimplified the working memory system, assuming it was a single component. By adding additional components to their model, Baddeley and Hitch were able to account for findings that single-component models struggled to explain.

Author's Aims

In writing "Working Memory," Alan D. Baddeley and Graham Hitch aimed to show observable evidence for the structure of short-term memory, detail exactly how it operates, and examine its function and purpose. They wrote, "We began with a very simple question: what is short-term memory for?"[1]

Baddeley and Hitch address these aims by first introducing the reader to the current state of research on short-term memory. They note that many researchers already assumed that short-term memory operates in some way as a working memory system. Such a system clearly doesn't just hold information, but actively determines what to do with it and then uses it for some purpose. Baddeley and Hitch argue that this assumption was not backed up with evidence: "It appears then, that STS [short-term store] constitutes a system for which great claims have been made by many workers (including the present authors), for which there is little good evidence."[2]

> 66 In attempting to assess the role of memory in any task, one is faced with a fundamental problem. What is meant by STS [short-term store]? 99
>
> Alan D. Baddeley and Graham Hitch, "Working Memory"

To address this concern, they detail the results of 10 original experiments. Each of these studies was intended to build up evidence to address previous concerns about short-term memory theories—for instance, the Atkinson–Shiffrin model.* Through a process of questioning existing assumptions and providing new evidence, Baddeley and Hitch build up a new, multicomponent theory of working memory. In conclusion, they write, "We hope that our preliminary attempts to begin answering the question will convince the reader, not necessarily that our views are correct, but that the question was, and is, well worth asking."[3] The fact that the Baddeley–Hitch model* displaced previous models and is still important today suggests they succeeded in this aim.

Approach

Before the publication of Baddeley and Hitch's "Working Memory," scholars often based memory* research on data from medical patients with memory problems. For instance, if a patient with brain damage in a certain area performed poorly on a memory task, they concluded that this specific part of the brain was essential for the performance of the task.

Baddeley and Hitch did not have access to brain-damaged patients. Instead, they used participants with normal brain functioning, but they employed a unique method to deplete the resources of certain memory functions. Decades later Baddeley recalled this innovative approach that was integral to the paper: "It seemed an inauspicious time to be entering the field of STM [short-term memory], given its problems and the fact that we did not have access to patients with the STM deficits that were so theoretically important. Happily, we hit on the idea of turning our students into 'patients,' not by removing chunks of their left hemisphere, but by keeping it occupied in remembering strings of digits, while performing the various tasks that were assumed to depend upon short-term/working memory. The longer the digit sequence, we argued, the more STM capacity should be used up and the greater the disruption."[4]

Prior research had found that people can only hold, on average, about six digits or pieces of information in their short-term storage* at a time.[5] Baddeley and Hitch relied on this, arguing that if participants had their short-term storage filled, it would be the same as using patients with damage to their short-term memory. This became a standard method in memory research, and the area was no longer reliant on a small number of brain-damaged patients with specific memory problems.

Contribution in Context

Baddeley and Hitch were not the first to come up with the idea of a working memory system—one that is actively involved in processing as well as storing short-term information. Computer science* scholars first popularized the concept, which earlier memory researchers, including Atkinson and Shiffrin,[6] then adopted. Baddeley and Hitch were in fact part of a growing school of thought that viewed short-term memory as active, dynamic, and involved in multiple aspects of cognition* and performance.

Baddeley and Hitch's mentors, R. Conrad* and Donald Broadbent,* possibly advanced their conclusion that working memory is a multicomponent system. Baddeley's interest in memory research developed while he was at the University of Cambridge, working under the supervision of both Conrad and Broadbent. Graham Hitch came through a similar network: Broadbent was his

PhD advisor, and through that connection Hitch became Baddeley's postdoctoral researcher in 1972.[7] It was with these mentors that Baddeley and Hitch first came across evidence for multiple components in memory.

In the 1960s, Conrad had found evidence that short- and long-term memory* have separate components that handle acoustic information (acquired through hearing, such as a street address). This research motivated Baddeley, and some of his early work on memory extends Conrad's original work. "However, Conrad had not tested other kinds of similarity," Baddeley recalls, "and so I decided I would use words rather than letters and compare acoustic similarity* with similarity of meaning [Conrad found that similar-sounding letters like *b* and *v* were more difficult for the short-term memory, relative to the long-term system]."[8]

NOTES

1 Alan D. Baddeley and Graham Hitch, "Working Memory," *Psychology of Learning and Motivation* 8 (1974): 86.

2 Baddeley and Hitch, "Working Memory," 49.

3 Baddeley and Hitch, "Working Memory," 86.

4 "Looking Back: How It All Began," *The Psychologist*, accessed June 5, 2015, https://thepsychologist.bps.org.uk/volume-28/april-2015/looking-back-how-it-all-began

5 George A. Miller, "The Magical Number Seven, Plus or Minus Two: Some Limits on Our Capacity for Processing Information," *Psychological Review* 63, no. 2 (1956): 81–97.

6 Richard C. Atkinson and Richard M. Shiffrin, *The Control Processes of Short-Term Memory*, Institute for Mathematical Studies in the Social Sciences (Stanford, CA: Stanford University, 1971).

7 Alan Baddeley, "Working Memory: Theories, Models, and Controversies," *Annual Review of Psychology* 63 (2012): 5.

8 "Looking Back," *The Psychologist*.

SECTION 2
IDEAS

MAIN IDEAS

KEY POINTS

- Baddeley and Hitch provide a new model of short-term memory* consisting of multiple components: a central processing component and two different components responsible for storing short-term information.

- The main argument of "Working Memory" is that a multiple component working memory* system is actively involved in the processing of short-term information.

- The authors built their argument through a series of experiments that test alternative explanations while establishing the multiple component structure of working memory. But the text often assumes a lot of knowledge on the part of the reader.

Key Themes

In "Working Memory," Alan D. Baddeley and Graham Hitch strive to provide observable evidence to shed light on the numerous conflicting existing models of short-term memory. They write that their "aim is to present a body of new experimental evidence which provides a firm basis for the working memory hypothesis."[1] In presenting the results of 10 original studies, they conclude that there is evidence for a working memory system with multiple components.

These conclusions, which establish a new structure of short-term memory, provide the main themes of "Working Memory":

- Working memory is not a single short-term store,* but rather a multiple component system.

> 66 Despite more than a decade of intensive research on the topic of short-term memory, we still know virtually nothing about its role in normal human information processing. 99
>
> Alan D. Baddeley and Graham Hitch, "Working Memory"

- This system contains a central processor for processing information that Baddeley and Hitch call the central executive.*
- It also contains two short-term stores: an articulatory component* for holding speech-based information and a visual component for holding visual/spatial information.

This model presents working memory as an active processor of information rather than a passive system of storage. Baddeley and Hitch write that "despite the frequency with which [short-term store] has been assigned this role as an operational or working memory, the empirical evidence for such a view is remarkably sparse."[2] Baddeley and Hitch also propose that the components of the model interact and are actively involved in other processes, such as learning and reasoning.

Exploring the Ideas
The authors' experiments required participants to perform two tasks at the same time—what is called a dual-task paradigm.* For instance, in assessing the role of working memory in reasoning, they asked participants to judge whether certain sentences were logical or grammatically correct. They showed participants, for example, the letters *BA* and then had them judge whether the sentence *B is followed by A* is correct or incorrect. While the participants were performing this reasoning task, the authors asked some of them to recite a list of

three digits and others a list of six digits.

According to the dominant view at the time, a short-term memory store* should have limited capacity. Previous research had suggested that people can hold between five and nine pieces of information in this short-term store.[3] Baddeley and Hitch assumed that participants reciting six digits would have their short-term store filled to capacity. "If the task relies on a limited-capacity system, then one might expect the additional load to impair performance."[4]

Yet participants whom the authors asked to recite six digits while performing this and other tasks made no more errors than those whom they asked to recite three digits or who didn't have to recite anything—although they did take slightly longer to perform the reasoning task. These findings suggest that the short-term store is *not* the system most responsible for performance on the reasoning task. Baddeley and Hitch concluded that an additional component must be involved in the reasoning task. As they write in "Working Memory": "There appears to be a considerable component of working memory which is not taken up by the digit span task [i.e., the recitation task]."[5]

This additional component, they reasoned, processes short-term information and makes decisions, and is responsible for determining if *B* follows *A* in the reasoning task described above. "We would like to suggest that the core of the working memory system consists of a limited-capacity 'work space' which can be divided between storage and control processing demands,"[6] they note in "Working Memory." They call this component the central executive* and argue that it acts as a central processor, processing information and controlling the action from both of the two short-term stores.

These two stores, Baddeley and Hitch argue, are involved in the storage of short-term information. One holds speech-based information (e.g. a series of digits). They refer to this as the articulatory component.* The more digits held in this component, the more slowly participants in their experiments performed in the reasoning task. But the effects were not large, and the participants did not make *more* errors—they were just *slower*. This suggests that this component has *some* involvement in reasoning, but it cannot be the *only* component of working memory involved in the task.

Baddeley and Hitch also describe in "Working Memory" a "separate peripheral memory component, based on the visual system."[7] They do not directly discuss this component in their text, but cite previous work by other researchers that had suggested its existence. They conclude: "It is clear that visual and auditory short-term storage do employ different subsystems."[8] Importantly, Baddeley and Hitch assume that two tasks *can* be carried out simultaneously as long as two different parts of the working memory system are involved in the two different tasks.

Language and Expression

"Working Memory" is not easily accessible to the general reader. Baddeley and Hitch wrote it primarily for academic psychologists studying human short-term memory. As such, it uses language specific to the field of memory research, makes references to other models of human memory without much explanation, and includes a lot of statistics.

Baddeley and Hitch also note that, in one sense, the paper is incomplete. "The reader will notice obvious gaps where further experiments clearly need to be performed," they write, "and it is more than probable that such experiments will modify to a greater or lesser degree our current tentative theoretical position." Baddeley and Hitch's intention is not just to provide a new model of memory, supported by data, but also to provide fellow memory researchers with new directions for research.

At the beginning of the paper, Baddeley and Hitch discuss the existing theory of short-term memory. They then present the results of 10 original experiments that slowly make the case for a multiple component system. Some of these studies depleted the short–term memory store by requiring participants to recite digits, as described above. Other studies had participants recite words, not digits. And still others had participants complete different tasks from the reasoning task described above. The authors detail how their findings from each of these studies have led to their conclusions and rule out alternative explanations. They also present the results of their experiments in tables and figures throughout the paper.

NOTES

1   Alan D. Baddeley and Graham Hitch, "Working Memory," *Psychology of Learning and Motivation* 8 (1974): 49.

2   Baddeley and Hitch, "Working Memory," 47-8.

3   George A. Miller, "The Magical Number Seven, Plus or Minus Two: Some Limits on Our Capacity for Processing Information," *Psychological Review* 63, no. 2 (1956): 81–97.

4   Baddeley and Hitch, "Working Memory," 51.

5   Baddeley and Hitch, "Working Memory," 75.

6   Baddeley and Hitch, "Working Memory," 75-6.

7   Baddeley and Hitch, "Working Memory," 81.

8   Baddeley and Hitch, "Working Memory," 80.

MODULE 6
SECONDARY IDEAS

KEY POINTS

- Baddeley and Hitch argue that working memory* is involved in several aspects of performance—including reasoning, reading comprehension, and learning. They also detail the relationship between working memory and the recency effect.*

- These secondary ideas, which are about the function and application of working memory, are aimed at memory researchers.

- Baddeley and Hitch provide some of the earliest and strongest observable evidence for the function of working memory in reasoning, reading comprehension, and learning.

Other Ideas

Alan D. Baddeley and Graham Hitch agreed with prominent memory researchers such as Richard C. Atkinson* and Richard M. Shiffrin* who believed in a working memory system that plays a role in learning and other aspects of human performance and cognition.* But they wanted to find observable evidence to demonstrate these assumptions. In "Working Memory" they ask, "Is there any evidence that the tasks of reasoning, comprehension, and learning share a common working memory system?"[1] By arguing that working memory is involved in all of reasoning, comprehension, and learning, Baddeley and Hitch also promote in the text the idea that working memory not only stores information, but also actively processes it. That is, most of what we mean by *thinking* involves working memory.

Another secondary idea in "Working Memory" concerns the

> ❝ Our experiments also suggest that working
> memory plays a part in verbal reasoning and in prose
> comprehension. ❞
>
> Alan D. Baddeley and Graham Hitch, "Working Memory"

recency effect: the tendency to recall information better if it was
presented more recently. For instance, when people are asked to
remember a list of 20 names they are unfamiliar with, they are better at
recalling the last couple of names than ones presented earlier in the list.
Prior to the publication of "Working Memory," researchers assumed
that the recency effect occurred because items presented last in a series
stay in the short-term store* while earlier items have gone into long-
term memory* or been forgotten. However, Baddeley and Hitch
found the recency effect in all studies, even when participants' short-
term stores were depleted and presumably unable to store even the
most recent information from a list.

Exploring the Ideas

All 10 original experiments that Baddeley and Hitch conducted rely
on the dual task paradigm,* and all involved a recitation task intended
to load the short-term store.* But the second task, designed to
measure performance, differed between studies. Sometimes it was a
reasoning task, as described earlier. But Baddeley and Hitch also
wanted to examine working memory's relationship to learning and
reading comprehension.

To test reading comprehension, they asked participants to "judge
whether a single sentence was impossible or possible."[2] For instance,
they had them choose whether the sentences, *Red headed Ned said Ted
fed in bed* and *Red headed Ned Ted said fed in bed* are grammatical or
ungrammatical. To test learning performance, Baddeley and Hitch

relied on participants' ability to recall information. For this task, they asked participants to remember a list of 10 or 16 words. Later, those participants had to recall as many of the words as they could.

Baddeley and Hitch's focus on these three areas—comprehension, reasoning, and learning—led them to conclude that a single working memory system was responsible. In "Working Memory" they write: "An attempt is made to apply comparable techniques in all three cases in the hope that this will allow a common pattern to emerge, if the same working memory system is operative in all three instances."[3] Further, they say, "There appears then to be a consistent pattern of effects across the three types of task studied, strongly suggesting the operation of a common system such as the working memory initially proposed."[4] Here they are referring to their finding that across these three tasks, performance was slower, but not less accurate, when participants were also forced to recite six digits.

Baddeley and Hitch expected the recency effect to disappear when participants recited six digits. Researchers previously assumed that the recency effect occurred because people were still rehearsing the latest items presented in a list in the short-term store (as when you recite something so you won't forget it). However, Baddeley and Hitch found that participants who had their short-term store filled with another task (reciting digits) still displayed the recency effect on the learning task. Thus, Baddeley and Hitch argue in "Working Memory" that the recency effect "reflects the operation of a retrieval strategy."[5] They suggest that more recent bits of information are tagged or marked as *recent* in memory and that people "may frequently access items on the basis of this cue."[6] A simplified analogy is to think of your memories like a stack of cards: when you try to recall something, your memory starts to grab at the cards on the top of the deck.

Overlooked

Baddeley and Hitch's interpretation of the recency effect was largely overlooked. The main idea of the paper, the multicomponent model of working memory, was not only novel, but also supported by the results of experiments. The authors' ideas about the recency effect were just speculation. In "Working Memory" they concede that whether cues that mark information as recent "can be used to retrieve other information, is an empirical question which remains unanswered."[7]

Writing in the 1990s, Baddeley and Hitch described the continued neglect of the recency effect: "It was a phenomenon of considerable interest and theoretical concern during the 1960s and features in most basic textbooks, but has in recent years been relatively neglected by both empirical researchers and by theorists."[8] They suggested that although progress on the recency effect was made in the decades following "Working Memory," the topic had been neglected because it was unattractive.

There is still no consensus regarding how the recency effect works. But experts generally agreed that the effect is more a result of a retrieval strategy, as Baddeley and Hitch first presumed, than how information is stored. Baddeley and Hitch echoed this point in the 1990s, noting that decades of "data argue strongly for an association between the recency effect and a retrieval strategy involving a last-in-first-out output order."[9] Rather than being a conscious strategy that people use, it seems that this is done automatically by our memory system.

NOTES

1   Alan D. Baddeley and Graham Hitch, "Working Memory," *Psychology of Learning and Motivation* 8 (1974): 49.

2   Baddeley and Hitch, "Working Memory," 63.

3   Baddeley and Hitch, "Working Memory," 49.

4   Baddeley and Hitch, "Working Memory," 75.

5   Baddeley and Hitch, "Working Memory," 84.

6   Baddeley and Hitch, "Working Memory," 84.

7   Baddeley and Hitch, "Working Memory," 85.

8   Alan D. Baddeley and Graham Hitch, "The Recency Effect: Implicit Learning with Explicit Retrieval?," *Memory & Cognition* 21, no. 2 (1993): 146.

9   Baddeley and Hitch, "Recency Effect," 152.

ACHIEVEMENT

KEY POINTS

- "Working Memory" provided original, observable evidence that supported a new model of working memory.

- Integral to this achievement was the research that people had gathered over the previous decade, enabled in part by the cognitive revolution* and its emphasis on the internal workings of the mind.

- When Baddeley and Hitch wrote their paper, the methods for accessing memory function were limited, which prevented them from further detailing their model.

Assessing the Argument

Alan D. Baddeley and Graham Hitch succeeded in their primary aim to provide observable evidence to explain the structure and purpose of short-term memory.* They shifted the focus of what short-term memory does to its active, working capabilities. Edward E. Smith,* Stephen Michael Kosslyn, and Lawrence W. Barsalou in their textbook, *Cognitive Psychology: Mind and Brain,* note, "The Baddeley–Hitch model* was a major departure from earlier theories about short-term memory in that it emphasized neither its duration nor its relationship to long-term memory, but rather its flexibility and critical importance to ongoing cognition."[1] The 10 experiments in "Working Memory," through which Baddeley and Hitch investigated the question "What is short-term memory for?"[2] effectively altered the focus of research on memory.

It was only through examining the function of short-term memory that Baddeley and Hitch settled on the structure of working

> **"** The Baddeley–Hitch model and the idea of a 'mental workspace' took us a long way in the exploration of working memory. **"**
>
> Edward E. Smith, Stephen Michael Kosslyn, and Lawrence W. Barsalou, *Cognitive Psychology: Mind and Brain*

memory. In fact, in 1974, they were still not convinced they had uncovered the true structure of working memory. Years later, Baddeley recalled his reluctance to publish "Working Memory," saying: "We hesitated; the model was clearly not yet complete (it still isn't!), but it seemed too good an opportunity to miss, and Baddeley and Hitch (1974) duly appeared."[3]

Achievement in Context

Baddeley and Hitch wrote "Working Memory" in the middle of the cognitive revolution in the 1970s—a time when psychologists were dedicated to the inner workings of the mind. This certainly encouraged the work's general acceptance. The paper would not have gained the same traction at the height of behaviorism* in the 1950s. Behaviorism as a discipline insisted on observable behavior. Memory itself was not observable, only the behaviors that resulted.

John B. Watson,* the founder of behaviorism, wrote about the study of memory, "The behaviorist, since he never uses the term 'memory,' is under no compulsion to attempt to define it."[4] He continued, "so, instead of using the term memory, the behaviorist speaks of how much skill has been retained and how much has been lost in a period of no practice. Our objection to the term memory is that it is shot through with all kinds of philosophical and subjective connotations."[5]

The cognitive revolution, however, ushered in a time when the *unobservable* workings of the mind were the focus. This was especially true of memory research; throughout the 1960s, cognitive psychologists began studying memory despite not being able to see what was going on in the brain.

Limitations

Baddeley and Hitch referred to brain structures that were not easily observable, but could have bolstered their arguments. For instance, were the different components they discussed associated with different areas of the brain? How or where in the brain do these components communicate with each other? Such questions were not part of their aims at the time. But finding answers to them would have strengthened their arguments for the structure of working memory.

Baddeley and Hitch's model, and others describing memory systems, intend to detail general memory functioning. That is, across cultures and time, such models try to outline the structure and function of working memory. Baddeley wrote about the evolutionary origins of memory: "My own conclusion after surveying the experimental literature and its implications for clinical and social psychology is that we [humans] have evolved an overall cognitive system that attempts to minimize the demands made on WM [working memory] while allowing it to intervene where necessary."[6]

That said, there are plenty of what psychologists call individual differences in memory ability. Different people have different capacities in their central executive* and two storage systems. Children, the elderly, Alzheimer's* patients, people with damage to brain structures responsible for memory—all these populations have different capabilities within one or more component in the Baddeley–Hitch model. But, as noted earlier, these groups of people actually make up an integral part of memory research.

NOTES

1   Edward E. Smith, Stephen Michael Kosslyn, and Lawrence W. Barsalou, *Cognitive Psychology: Mind and Brain* (Upper Saddle River, NJ: Pearson Prentice Hall, 2007).

2   Alan D. Baddeley and Graham Hitch, "Working Memory." *Psychology of Learning and Motivation* 8 (1974): 86.

3   "Looking Back: How it All Began," *The Psychologist*, accessed June 5, 2015, https://thepsychologist.bps.org.uk/volume-28/april-2015/looking-back-how-it-all-began

4   John B. Watson, *Behaviorism*. (New York: W. W. Norton & Company, Inc., 1925), 220.

5   Watson, *Behaviorism*, 223.

6   Alan Baddeley, "Working Memory: Theories, Models, and Controversies," *Annual Review of Psychology* 63 (2012): 24.

PLACE IN THE AUTHOR'S WORK

KEY POINTS

- 1974's "Working Memory" was an early work in Baddeley's long career studying memory.

- Baddeley dedicated much of his career toward advancing the working memory* model, and the framework for this work traces back to "Working Memory."

- Baddeley remains best known for "Working Memory." His publications in 1992 and 2000 confirm and update the original model.

Positioning

"Working Memory" is an early work of both Alan D. Baddeley and Graham Hitch. The text is integral to their careers as it describes the original version of their model of working memory,* which they continue to refine. Both spent time on memory research before this 1974 publication—Baddeley beginning in the late 1960s and Hitch during the early 1970s. They both still publish literature on memory.

Baddeley, in particular, has refined the original Baddeley–Hitch working memory model.* For instance, in a 1992 paper, also titled "Working Memory," he summarized some of the research developments that support or question the original model.[1] This paper has been even more widely cited than the original 1974 paper. Then, in 2000, Baddeley updated the original model, adding a further component.[2]

Baddeley and Hitch did not believe their 1974 paper was a completed model of working memory. Many of their assumptions were not based on direct evidence. For instance, they suggested that a spatial/visual storage component existed, but they did so based on a

> **❝ The model was presented in an invited chapter in 1974 (Baddeley & Hitch, 1974) and has continued to drive the work of both Baddeley and Hitch since that time. ❞**
> American Psychological Association Awards for Distinguished Scientific Contributions

combination of logic and findings from other researchers.

In the decades following "Working Memory," the working memory model has been modified not only Baddeley himself, but also the many researchers basing their work on the Baddeley–Hitch working memory model. The main ideas, however, are still the same. The model remains one with multiple components, but the two short-term stores have acquired new labels, and the central processor has been further specified.

Integration

Baddeley's academic career has focused on memory research and specifically the idea of a working memory system. A popular textbook in cognitive psychology* states that "In the years since his first work on the model, Alan Baddeley has been a major figure in working memory research, continuing to elaborate on the initial conception of the working memory model and providing a great deal of experimental support for its validity and usefulness."[3]

The 1974 publication of "Working Memory" can be seen as the first work to detail a multicomponent system of working memory. While a simplification, the next 25 years essentially tested, refuted, and confirmed this 1974 model. In Baddeley's view, this original model has held up well against the results of decades of testing. In 2000, he wrote: "Over the 25 years since the publication of our initial paper, the concept of working memory (WM) has proved to be surprisingly durable."[4]

Baddely detailed the confirmations and minor adjustments to the model in his 1992 paper "Working Memory." In it, he concludes: "The concept of a working memory system that temporarily stores information as part of the performance of complex cognitive tasks is proving to be productive."[5] Much of this 1992 publication describes how subsequent research confirmed much of the original 1974 working memory model. Baddeley was confident this model would continue to serve the field well, writing, "If these links [between the model's components] can be sustained and developed, the concept of working memory is likely to continue to be a fruitful one."[6]

In 2000, Baddeley, still working from the original model, made his first significant change, adding a fourth component to the working memory model: the episodic buffer,* which is controlled and monitored by the central executive.* The episodic buffer is responsible for integrating and linking different formats of information (for example, visual and verbal). Baddeley admitted, "There have always been phenomena that did not fit comfortably within the Baddeley and Hitch model, particularly in its more recent form."[7] This was the motivation for adding a fourth component.

Significance

It is reasonable to say that the 1974 publication of "Working Memory" is Baddeley's most important and best work. His updated 1992 publication by the same title would become more widely cited, but it mostly serves as a confirmation of the original work. In the years between the two publications, Baddeley became a leading memory researcher and has remained the key figure behind the dominant working memory model. Throughout his career, he has written over 600 publications, including 11 books, and most of this work is on memory. The idea most attributable to him is still the multicomponent working memory model that he developed with Hitch.

Since the publication of "Working Memory," Baddeley has

cemented his place as the leading advocate of a working memory model. Cognitive psychology textbooks often have at least one chapter dedicated to working memory, and that chapter will usually focus on Baddeley and the Baddeley–Hitch model. Research interest in working memory has grown, as Baddeley himself noted in 2012:"The topic of working memory has increased dramatically in citation counts since the early years, not all of course related to or supportive of my own work, but a recent attempt to review it ended with more than 50 pages of references."[8] It is not surprising that it is Baddeley who is often requested to supply such reviews, because he is still the most prolific researcher in the field.

NOTES

1   Alan Baddeley, "Working Memory," *Science* 255, no. 5044 (1992): 556–9.

2   Alan Baddeley, "The Episodic Buffer: A New Component of Working Memory?," *Trends in Cognitive Sciences* 4, no. 11 (2000): 417–23.

3   Edward E. Smith, Stephen Michael Kosslyn, and Lawrence W. Barsalou, *Cognitive Psychology: Mind and Brain* (Upper Saddle River, NJ: Pearson Prentice Hall, 2007), 250.

4   Baddeley, "Episodic Buffer," 417.

5   Baddeley, "Working Memory," 559.

6   Baddeley, "Working memory," 559.

7   Baddeley, "Episodic buffer," 417.

8   Alan Baddeley, "Working Memory: Theories, Models, and Controversies," *Annual Review of Psychology* 63 (2012): 2.

SECTION 3
IMPACT

MODULE 9
THE FIRST RESPONSES

KEY POINTS

- Two common and foreseeable criticisms of "Working Memory" involved how the visual/spatial store component* stores information.

- Questions also arose about the differences of the role of the central executive* in attention and storage.

- Baddeley accepted findings from other researchers that added new detail to the original working memory model,* and he was largely receptive and accommodating to new research examining the Baddeley–Hitch model.*

Criticism

One clear and anticipated criticism revolved around the visual/spatial component of working memory* that Alan D. Baddeley and Graham Hitch proposed. Having reported and examined the verbal component and storage system, they concluded without much evidence that a similar system exists for visual and spatial information. As they say in "Working Memory": "It seems probable that a comparable system exists for visual memory which is different at least in part from the [verbal] system we have been discussing."[1]

Many aspects of this visual/spatial system were undefined and then questioned after "Working Memory" was published. Was information in this system primarily stored visually or spatially? In this context, "visual" referred to *what* information (such as color, shape, or size), while "spatial" refers to *where* information (such as the location and positioning of objects and movements). Baddeley recalls, "Results convinced me that the system was essentially spatial. Robert Logie,*

> ❝ The success of such a framework should be based, as suggested by Lakatos (1976), not only on its capacity to explain existing data but also on its productivity in generating good, tractable questions linked to empirical methods that can be widely applied. ❞
>
> Alan D. Baddeley, "Working Memory: Theories, Models, and Controversies"

who was working with me at the time, disagreed and set out to show that I was wrong."[2] As an example, Logie, a cognitive psychologist and professor at the University of Edinburgh, showed that the words *cow* and *chair* could be memorized—and therefore stored visually—if participants memorized a visual interaction of the two, such as a cow sitting in a chair.

Another major area of debate involved Baddeley and Hitch's conception of the central executive component. Their description of it was limited yet, they argued, it was capable of performing many tasks. In particular, they noted its role in attention and tasks that required attention, such as counting backwards.

While accepting the foundation of the Baddeley–Hitch multicomponent model, memory researchers Meredyth Daneman* and Patricia A. Carpenter* questioned the central executive's ability to both process and store information. They argued that the recitation tasks that Baddeley and Hitch used to deplete the *storage* component of working memory were not effective at depleting the *processing* and *attentional* components. Daneman and Carpenter tried "to devise a measure that taxed both the processing and storage functions of working memory."[3] They came up with a task where participants read a series of sentences and have to remember the final words of each sentence while they are reading.

Responses

After publication of the 1974 text, Baddeley quickly changed the name of the visual/spatial component to the visuo-spatial sketchpad.* That renaming, he wrote, left "open the issue of whether it [the storage of information] was basically visual, spatial, or both." Baddeley believed that information was stored spatially in this component, but he accepted Logie's findings and concluded that the sketchpad can handle both visual and spatial information and does so separately. Baddeley recalls, "There are now multiple demonstrations of the dissociation of visual and spatial WM [working memory]."[4] Though Logie disagreed with Baddeley on this and other issues over the following decades, they developed a fruitful collaboration, publishing several articles and chapters on working memory.

After Daneman and Carpenter questioned the function of the central executive, Baddeley adopted their working memory task—for example, having participants recall the final words in a series of sentences.[5] Daneman and Carpenter concluded, "Individual differences in reading comprehension may reflect differences in working memory capacity [measured by their new reading task], specifically in the trade-off between its processing and storage functions."[6] Baddeley accepted this task as a legitimate test of the central executive's capabilities, later recalling that "such results were gratifying in demonstrating the practical significance of WM [working memory]."[7]

Reviewing the literature on working memory in 2012, Baddeley remarked that Daneman and Carpenter's findings and their working memory task were an important advancement for the field. "This and similar tests that require the combination of temporary storage and processing have proved enormously successful in predicting performance on cognitive tasks ranging from comprehension to complex reasoning and from learning a programming language to resisting distraction."[8]

Conflict and Consensus

What started out as conflicts in models did eventually reach consensus. Baddeley incorporated the findings of Logie, Daneman, Carpenter, and others into newer conceptualizations of working memory. That should not be surprising, given the tentativeness with which Baddeley and Hitch first proposed the model in 1974. In particular, Baddeley has held that the central executive and visuo-spatial sketchpad are more difficult to study than the articulatory component,* which he relabeled the phonological loop.* In fact, Baddeley seems willing to incorporate the findings of other researchers when they add to the Baddeley–Hitch multicomponent model, and he and Hitch have not only welcomed new research findings, but have also actively invited them. His long-standing collaboration with Logie and his references to Daneman and Carpenter are examples.

Baddeley has, however, been less accommodating of views that run completely counter to the Baddeley–Hitch multicomponent model. For instance, he did not further consider single-component models such as the Atkinson–Shiffrin model,* nor did "Working Memory" prompt a debate over the merits of single- versus multicomponent models of working memory.

Baddeley preferred alterations to how the Baddeley–Hitch model worked over calls to change the content of components. He believed that although the original model was in need of additional research, there was enough evidence to support multiple components. Baddeley and Hitch concluded "Working Memory" by writing, "Further experiments clearly need to be performed, and it is more than probable that such experiments will modify to a greater or lesser degree our current tentative theoretical position."[9]

NOTES

1   Alan D. Baddeley and Graham Hitch, "Working Memory," *Psychology of Learning and Motivation* 8 (1974): 80.

2   Alan Baddeley, "Working Memory: Theories, Models, and Controversies," *Annual Review of Psychology* 63 (2012): 13.

3   Meredyth Daneman and Patricia A. Carpenter, "Individual Differences in Working Memory and Reading," *Journal of Verbal Learning and Verbal Behavior* 19, no. 4 (1980): 451.

4   Baddeley, "Theories," 13.

5   Alan Baddeley, Robert Logie, Ian Nimmo-Smith, and Neil Brereton, "Components of Fluent Reading," *Journal of Memory and Language* 24, no. 1 (1985): 119–31.

6   Daneman and Carpenter, "Individual differences," 451.

7   Baddeley, "Theories," 15.

8   Baddeley, "Theories," 15.

9   Baddeley and Hitch, "Working Memory," 49.

MODULE 10
THE EVOLVING DEBATE

KEY POINTS

- In 2000, Baddeley added the episodic buffer* as the fourth component of his working memory* model.

- The working memory model has become integrated into work in neuropsychology* and research on conscious* awareness.

- The Baddeley–Hitch model* and the dual-task paradigm* used in "Working Memory" are influential in other disciplines of psychology—such as developmental psychology,* where researchers use the model to assess children's abilities and impairments.

Uses and Problems

Memory researchers accepted the three components of working memory that Alan D. Baddeley and Graham Hitch originally proposed in 1974. Other scholars then put much effort into elaborating on the details of those components. Within a few years, Robert Logie* helped lead work on how information was stored in the visuo-spatial sketchpad,* and Meredyth Daneman* and Patricia A. Carpenter* began research on the function of the central executive.* Scholars carried out further studies into the specifics of each of the three components of the original Baddeley–Hitch model.

Over the next two decades, issues arose that could not be answered by the original model, so Baddeley added a fourth component called the episodic buffer. The central executive controls that buffer, as it does the phonological loop* and visuo-spatial sketchpad. The episodic buffer is responsible for integrating and linking different forms of

❝ Inner speech is one of the most important modes of experience. Most of us go around the world talking to ourselves … there are many hundreds of experiments in the cognitive literature on verbal short-term memory, which is roughly the domain in which we rehearse telephone numbers, consider different ideas, and talk to ourselves generally (e.g. Baddeley, 1976). ❞

Bernard J. Baars,* *A Cognitive Theory of Consciousness*

information (for example, visual and verbal). In a 2000 article, Baddeley wrote, "There is a clear need, therefore, to assume a process or mechanism for synergistically combining information from various subsystems into a form of temporary representation."[1]

Numerous issues and publications led to this addition. One such was research surrounding prose recall.* Baddeley described the issue as follows: "If asked to recall a sequence of unrelated words, subjects typically begin to make errors once the number of words exceeds five or six. However, if the words comprise a meaningful sentence, then a span of 16 or more is possible."[2]

This process is called chunking.* It reflects our memory's ability to recall *meaningful* information more easily than *random* information. This chunking process requires working memory to interact with long-term memory* to determine the meaning of the chunks or sentences. To account for where this chunking is stored and used by working memory, Baddeley argued the model needed "a store that is capable of drawing information both from the slave systems* [the phonological loop and the visuo-spatial sketchpad] and from LTM [long-term memory], and holding it in some integrated form."[3] He proposed the episodic buffer as a system that does just that.

Schools of Thought

From the beginning, working memory relied on neuropsychology,* particularly in patients with cognitive problems that often resulted from brain damage. This was also true of the development of the episodic buffer. For instance, in "Working Memory," Baddeley describes a patient with a normal functioning long-term memory but with a short-term memory* that is so damaged that she cannot recall an unrelated series of words. This suggests that her phonological loop*—the component responsible for storing and rehearsing verbal information—is damaged. However, she is better at recalling verbal information if it is chunked. Baddeley concludes, "This leaves a back-up store interpretation as the simplest interpretation."[4]

In other words, the episodic buffer acts as an additional component that is involved in the storage of information that is integrated between components, such as chunking. For instance, chunking requires communication between short- and long-term memory to attach meaning to a new chunk of information. Baddeley argued that these chunks are created and stored in the episodic buffer.

His working memory research has, in turn, influenced neuro-psychology. It is now a useful method for understanding and diagnosing patients with neurological impairments. Notably, tasks developed to measure working memory can be used to predict and diagnose Alzheimer's disease,* a degenerative brain disease marked by loss of memory.

Working memory also influences schools of thought on consciousness,* the state of being aware of oneself and one's surroundings. Baddeley wrote in 2000, "Although the question of conscious awareness was not tackled directly, the WM [working memory] model was implicitly assumed to play a role in consciousness."[5] The development of the episodic buffer, according to Baddeley, further clarified the relationship between consciousness and working memory. This is partly because the episodic buffer, which integrates information between long-term memory and working memory, is assumed to occur with conscious awareness. Baddeley wrote, "This results in a theory of consciousness that resembles that proposed by [Bernard J.] Baars (1988), which assumes that consciousness serves as a mechanism for binding stimulus features into perceived objects."

In Current Scholarship

Today, the Baddeley–Hitch working memory model has several disciples. Chief among them is Hitch himself, who continues his own work detailing the functions of the components of the system. Also important is British psychologist Susan Gathercole,* who has collaborated with Baddeley. Much of Gathercole's work applies the Baddeley–Hitch working memory model to the study of children's cognitive deficits* or impairments to their cognitive ability. She often tests children's working memory capacities, sometimes using the dual-task paradigm, to assess and predict children's abilities in other performance areas.

For instance, after she collaborated with Baddeley in 1990, they discovered that "children selected as being developmentally language-disordered have a selective impairment in immediate phonological memory, whether tested by recall of word lists or by repetition of non-words" and "that phonological memory makes an important contribution to the development of many complex linguistic abilities in children."[6] Gathercole is now director of the Medical Research Council's Cognition and Brain Sciences Unit at the University of Cambridge—the Applied Psychology Unit where Baddeley began his career as a memory researcher.

NOTES

1   Alan Baddeley, "The Episodic Buffer: A New Component of Working Memory?," *Trends in Cognitive Sciences* 4, no. 11 (2000): 421.

2   Baddeley, "Episodic Buffer," 419.

3   Baddeley, "Episodic Buffer," 421.

4   Baddeley, "Episodic Buffer," 419.

5   Baddeley, "Episodic Buffer," 420.

6   Susan E. Gathercole and Alan D. Baddeley, "Phonological Memory Deficits in Language Disordered Children: Is There a Causal Connection?," *Journal of Memory and Language* 29, no. 3 (1990): 358.

IMPACT AND INFLUENCE TODAY

KEY POINTS

- "Working Memory" and the Baddeley–Hitch model* remain the dominant view of working memory.
- Baddeley is cautious of neuroimaging* techniques that attempt to find specific regions of the brain that represent working memory components and other regions associated with memory processes.
- Some memory researchers, drawing from the Atkinson–Shiffrin model* of the 1960s, argue that multiple components are not necessary to explain many of the phenomena found in memory research.

Position

"Baddeley's conceptualization of working memory is still highly influential and serves as a source of an enormous amount of research,"[1] note the authors of a popular cognitive psychology textbook. The original three components of working memory* that Alan D. Baddeley and Graham Hitch proposed are still part of the dominant view of working memory. Research over the past four decades has established some of the details of how these components work—information that was either absent or just speculation in their 1974 publication.

The Baddeley–Hitch model has influenced several areas of psychology where memory plays a role—for instance, in neuropsychology* and developmental psychology* in the work of such scholars as Susan Gathercole*). Further, doctors still use the working memory model, as well as the methods associated with it such as the dual-task paradigm,* with clinical patients with cognitive impairments.

> ❝ For the years 1980 to 2006, of the 16,154 papers that cited 'working memory' in their titles or abstracts, fully 7,339 included citations to Alan Baddeley. ❞
>
> John Jonides et al., "The Mind and Brain of Short-Term Memory"

The working memory model has also been important in research on the effect of drugs on cognitive abilities. As Edward Smith and his coauthor note in *Cognitive Psychology: Mind and Brain,* "Given the critical role of working memory in cognition,* it is of clinical importance to determine whether there might be any drug treatments that could improve working memory in such populations."[2]

Baddeley has speculated on a reason for the continued acceptance and broad application of the Baddeley–Hitch model. He wrote in 2012, "My own view is that this breadth of application has reflected the simplicity of the theoretical framework together with the availability of a few basic methodologies."[3]

Interaction

As new researchers begin studying memory, often applying new methods for the study of both the brain and the mind, they are reexamining some of the theories that Baddeley and Hitch describe in "Working Memory." This may be most obvious in neuroimaging research, which in part seeks to produce a map of the brain and uncover the functions of various brain areas, including memory.

As noted in a textbook discussing the issue, "Findings in both neuroimaging studies in humans and neural recording studies in monkeys suggest that the prefrontal cortex [an area in the front of the brain] is an important component of working memory."[4] Other neuroimaging studies have made more detailed inroads, uncovering specific brain regions associated with the components of working memory and even regions linked to specific processes, such as rehearsing words in the phonological loop.*

Baddeley, however, is cautious about the influence of current neuroimaging-based approaches to studying working memory. He recently wrote:"Although

I think it is very important to understand the neurobiological basis of WM [working memory], I am not yet convinced that it has made a major contribution to psychological theories of WM. This does not reflect a general rejection of neuroimaging, which offers an essential and potentially powerful tool for understanding cognition and its neural basis."

Baddeley continued, spelling out his concerns:"In the case of WM, however, I have two major sources of doubt. The first concerns the lack of apparent replicability [ability of studies to reproduce research findings] in the field. The second more basic concern is the validity of the assumption that anatomical localization [the mapping of brain regions] will provide a firm theoretical basis for a system as complex as WM in the absence of a much better understanding of the temporal structure of activation than is typically available at present."[5]

John Jonides,* a leading proponent of integrating neuroimaging methods with traditional approaches to studying memory, seems to agree that neuroimaging still has some way to go, but that it has been helpful in uncovering findings that would not be available otherwise. He admits in a recent review, "The points of contact among these different methods of studying STM [short-term memory] have multiplied over the past several years. As we have pointed out, significant and exciting challenges in furthering this integration lie ahead."[6]

The Continuing Debate

The role of neuroimaging in memory research, however, is relatively new. Some researchers and other readers who were originally challenged by the 1974 text continue their debate. For instance, Jeroen

G.W. Raaijmakers* and Richard Shiffrin* (the latter of the Atkinson–Shiffrin model that predated Baddeley and Hitch) developed an updated single component model of short-term memory around 1980 and continued to advance this model throughout the remainder of the century. In defending a single component model of working memory, Raaijmakers wrote, "The treatment of this model in textbooks on memory suggests that it has serious deficiencies. However, this assessment is quite wrong, and the two-store model [one for short-term memory, one for long-term memory, as in the Atkinson–Shiffrin model] is in fact capable of handling the findings that supposedly reject it."[7]

He argues that the Atkinson–Shiffrin model should not be viewed as a system of a single store each for short- and long-term memory.* Instead, people should consider it as a general model of all memory that distinguishes between structure and process. "The framework that Atkinson and Shiffrin proposed was based on a distinction between permanent structural features of the memory system and control processes. The permanent structural features include the various memory stores: the sensory registers (e.g. iconic and echoic memory) [visual and auditory memory], STS [short-term store]* and LTS [long-term store].* The other aspects that Atkinson and Shiffrin discussed were the control processes, the operations that are carried out to operate on and control memory, such as rehearsal, coding, and retrieval strategies."[8] Raaijmakers and Shiffrin and others argue that updated versions of these models are still helpful in studying memory.

NOTES

1   Edward E. Smith, Stephen Michael Kosslyn, and Lawrence W. Barsalou, *Cognitive Psychology: Mind and Brain* (Upper Saddle River, NJ: Pearson Prentice Hall, 2007), 250.

2   Smith, Kosslyn, and Barsalou, *Cognitive Psychology*, 276.

3   Alan Baddeley, "Working Memory: Theories, Models, and Controversies," *Annual Review of Psychology* 63 (2012): 24.

4   Smith, Kosslyn, and Barsalou, *Cognitive Psychology*, 260.

5   Baddeley, "Theories," 19.

6   John Jonides, Richard L. Lewis, Derek Evan Nee, Cindy A. Lustig, Marc G. Berman, and Katherine Sledge Moore, "The Mind and Brain of Short-Term Memory," *Annual Review of Psychology* 59 (2008): 216.

7   Jeroen G. W. Raaijmakers, "The Story of the Two-Store Model of Memory: Past Criticisms, Current Status, and Future Directions," in *Attention and Performance XIV (Silver Jubilee volume)*, ed. David E. Meyer and Sylvan Kornblum (Cambridge, MA: MIT Press, 1993), 467.

8   Raaijimakers, "Two-Store," 470.

WHERE NEXT?

KEY POINTS

- The Baddeley–Hitch working memory* model will likely assist in the understanding of other aspects of human cognition,* such as problem solving.

- With the use of new methods such as neuroimaging,* many of the original and adapted conclusions from the text are up for re-examination.

- The Baddeley–Hitch model remains the dominant framework of working memory.

Potential

Although the original Baddeley–Hitch working memory model published in 1974's "Working Memory" has been modified and added to—particularly with Baddeley's 2000 addition of the episodic buffer*—the core idea of a multicomponent system remains influential. One of the greatest assets of the model is that it can easily be modified. As Baddeley himself has argued, the model "might better be regarded as a simple theory [...], linking together existing knowledge and encouraging further investigation."[1]

Moreover, since the model's original conception, Baddeley has openly invited debate. The model and the decades of research that followed have led to our current understanding of working memory. But some believe that much still remains to be uncovered.

For instance, psychologists David Z. Hambrick* and Randall W. Engle* state: "Baddeley and Hitch (1974) began their chapter by commenting on the dearth of evidence concerning the role of short-term memory in normal information processing. We end this chapter

> 66 As we begin to fill in the empty spaces on the theoretical map, it hopefully will be increasingly possible to develop interlinked and more detailed models of the components of WM and their mode of interaction. 99
>
> Alan D. Baddeley, "Working Memory: Theories, Models, and Controversies"

by asking whether the same can be said of working memory: After nearly three decades of research on working memory, have we made progress toward understanding the role of working memory in higher level cognition? The answer appears to be yes and no."[2]

They continue: "First consider the 'yes' part of the answer. There is a considerable amount of evidence concerning the role of working memory in comprehension and reasoning." This was of course a stated intent of the original Baddeley and Hitch text. But Hambrick and Engle leave room for future research: "Now consider the 'no' part of the answer. Very little is known about the role of working memory in tasks traditionally studied in research on problem solving."[3] The fact that they anticipate working memory will play a role in tasks such as problem solving illustrates its potential as a framework for explaining other areas of psychology.

Future Directions

Meanwhile, over the past four decades, the model's influence has spread to other areas of psychology—such as developmental psychology* (how and why human behavior and mind change over a lifespan) and computational psychology* (where mathematical and computer-based models are created intending to mimic psychological processes).

But the field where the text may still have the most continued development and influence is neuroscience,* the biological study of the nervous system. Baddeley has been cautious in judging the influence of neuroimaging* methods so far, but this is an indication of the work that is still likely to be done.

For instance, John Jonides,* who examines memory with a neuroscientific approach, wrote of research in the early twenty-first century, "The past 10 years have brought near-revolutionary changes in psychological theories about short-term memory,* with similarly great advances in the neurosciences."[4]

Some of the leading researchers in this field, such as Tor D. Wager* and Edward E. Smith,* acknowledge that Baddeley first posed some of the early questions that neuroscientists later tackled. They wrote in a review of neuroscientific findings on working memory, "Some of the earliest neuroimaging studies of WM [working memory] addressed questions raised in part by Baddeley's (1992) framework—particularly, how the putative components of WM map onto brain systems and whether patterns of brain activation respect the distinctions between types of WM apparent in behavioral studies."[5] As neuroscience allows new insights into the structure, processing, and function of working memory, it is likely to have an increasing role in the study of memory.

Summary

"Working Memory" provides the origins and framework of the still-dominant model of working memory. It presents the view that short-term memory is more than a simple filing cabinet of memories, but is actively involved in reasoning, reading comprehension, and learning. The text also provides a concise overview of the short-term memory models that preceded it, such as the popular Atkinson–Shiffrin model* and the influential work of Fergus I. M. Craik* and Robert S. Lockhart.*

Readers may also view "Working Memory" as an entry point into studying human memory. In 2000, Baddeley added a fourth component to the model: the episodic buffer.[6] Given the dominance of the model since 1974, and the importance of memory in the field of cognitive psychology* and psychology more broadly, a wealth of research has further examined and extended the Baddeley–Hitch model. The model has also sparked research in other areas of psychology, like developmental psychology, and even in medicine, such as in relation to dementia-inducing diseases like Alzheimer's.* And today, methods unavailable in the 1970s, such as neuroimaging, are providing new insight into the workings of the Baddeley–Hitch model. The idea and the model are as relevant as ever, and "Working Memory" is the seminal read on the topic.

NOTES

1   Alan Baddeley, "Working Memory: Theories, Models, and Controversies," *Annual Review of Psychology* 63 (2012): 7.

2   David Z. Hambrick and Randall W. Engle, "The Role of Working Memory in Problem Solving," *The Psychology of Problem Solving* (2003): 200.

3   Hambrick and Engle, "Problem Solving," 201.

4   John Jonides, Richard L. Lewis, Derek Evan Nee, Cindy A. Lustig, Marc G. Berman, and Katherine Sledge Moore, "The Mind and Brain of Short-Term Memory," *Annual Review of Psychology* 59 (2008): 193.

5   Tor D. Wager and Edward E. Smith, "Neuroimaging Studies of Working Memory," *Cognitive, Affective, & Behavioral Neuroscience* 3, no. 4 (2003): 255.

6   Ian Baddeley, "The Episodic Buffer: A New Component of Working Memory?," *Trends in Cognitive Sciences* 4, no. 11 (2000): 417–23.

GLOSSARY

GLOSSARY OF TERMS

Acoustic similarity effect: a phenomenon whereby information that sounds similar (for example, a sequence of letters *b, g, e*) is more difficult to remember than a list of letters that sound different.

Alzheimer's disease: a disease that involves the degeneration of the brain. It is not yet curable or reversible. It is marked by dementia and loss of short-term memory.

Atkinson–Shiffrin model: a theoretical model of memory that Richard C. Atkinson and Richard M. Shiffrin detailed in a 1968 publication. It was the dominant model of memory before Alan D. Baddeley and Graham Hitch's 1974 text. It is one of the first works to distinguish between short- and long-term memory, and it views short-term memory as a single component.

Articulatory component: one component of the Baddeley–Hitch model of working memory. Specifically, this was the early name for the phonological loop: the component that stores and handles verbal and acoustic information.

Baddeley–Hitch model: a model of short-term/working memory that Alan D. Baddeley and Graham Hitch first described in "Working Memory" in 1974. This model argues for a multiple component structure of working memory that is involved in several aspects of cognition.

Behaviorism/behaviorist: a major theory of learning that dominated psychology throughout the twentieth century, particularly in the middle of the century. The theory tended to view cognitive factors like thinking as less relevant than behavior, and it advocated studying observable behaviors.

Central executive: one component of the Baddeley–Hitch working memory mode. It is involved in attention, and the control and regulation of the other short-term memory components.

Chunking: a method used by short-term memory to group pieces of information together into larger pieces that are more meaningful and therefore easier to remember.

Cognitive/Cognition: all mental abilities and processes associated with knowledge. The term includes memory, attention, problem-solving, learning, and others.

Cognitive deficits: impairments of cognitive ability. Such impairments may be the result of chronic conditions such as a brain injury, acute conditions such as poisoning or drugs, or developmental issues such as mental retardation.

Cognitive psychology: an area of psychology that examines basic mental processes such as memory, language, attention, and perception.

Cognitive revolution: the name of a broad movement beginning in the 1950s in several fields, such as psychology, anthropology, and linguistics. This movement focused on studying the internal thoughts, attitudes, motivations, and values that people use to make sense of and interact with the world.

Compositor: a term primarily used in the days of traditional printing for an individual who organizes a machine that sets the type for the printing press.

Computational psychology: involves creating mathematical and computer-based models intended to mimic psychological processes.

Computer science: the study of computing and automating processes on computers.

Conditioned response: an integral mechanism through which behaviorists argue learning occurs. It is a behavior that is learned through association with other events—for instance, people may develop taste aversions (i.e. a conditioned response) to foods if they previously got sick around the same time as they ate those same particular foods.

Conscious/consciousness: the state of being aware of oneself and one's surroundings. It was traditionally a topic of inquiry within philosophy, but is now situated within psychology and other sciences.

Developmental psychology: the study of how and why human behavior and the mind change over a lifespan.

Dual-task paradigm: a task that researchers primarily use in experiments in psychology where participants perform two tasks at the same time. The researchers then typically compare the performance of those participants with participants in situations where they perform tasks individually.

Episodic buffer: the fourth component of the Baddeley–Hitch working memory model. The central executive monitors and controls it, as it does the phonological loop and visuo-spatial sketchpad. The episodic buffer is responsible for integrating and linking different formats of information (e.g. visual and verbal).

Information theory: a branch of mathematics, engineering, and computer science. It is involved in quantifying information and concerned with how data (often computational data) is stored and travels between devices.

Long-term memory: considered to be the final stage of memory. It can store information for long periods of time, theoretically indefinitely.

Memory: in psychology, the mental encoding (perception and processing), storage (creating a record), and retrieval (calling back/recalling/remembering) of information.

Neuroimaging: techniques for acquiring images of the structure and function of the nervous system (e.g. the brain).

Neuropsychology: the study of the brain and nervous system's structure and function—in particular, how these systems relate to cognition and behavior.

Neuroscience: the biological study of the nervous system.

Phonological loop: one of the components in the Baddeley–Hitch working memory model. It is responsible for the short-term storing of verbal/acoustic information and for its short-term rehearsal (for example, repeating a phone number to prevent forgetting).

Postdoctoral fellow: a person who has received a doctoral degree and is currently involved in mentored research.

Prose recall: the recall of information in prose with a meaningful, grammatical structure. In relation to memory, it describes how people can more easily recall coherent sentences than random words.

Recency effect: the persistent finding in memory research that people more easily remember and recall items presented last.

Reinforcement: a principle component of behaviorism. It refers to a consequence (e.g. getting a good grade) that strengthens an association between behavior (e.g. studying) and a stimulus or cause (e.g. knowing a test is upcoming).

Short-term memory: the capacity to hold small amounts of information in mind for a number of seconds. It is often used interchangeably with the term "working memory," although it is helpful to think of working memory as a specific model of short-term memory.

Slave systems: Baddeley originally used this term to refer to the phonological loop and the visuo-spatial sketchpad in the sense that they are "slaves" to the central executive. (In other words, the central executive controls them.) The term has fallen out of favor.

Store/storage (memory store): the storage of information is one primary function of memory, and stores refer to structures or components of the brain that actually hold information and memories. Both short- and long-term memory have stores. Further, within the working memory model, each component is capable of storage.

Visuo-spatial sketchpad: one of the components in the Baddeley Hitch working memory model. It is responsible for the short-term storage and manipulation of information that we see.

Working memory: a system that is not only responsible for holding information in memory for a short period of time, but also for engaging in complex thought, learning new material, and accessing knowledge from long-term memory. It refers to the most prominent model of short-term memory.

World War II (1939–45): global war between the vast majority of world states, including all the great powers of the time.

PEOPLE MENTIONED IN THE TEXT

Richard C. Atkinson (b. 1929) is an American psychologist and former director of the National Science Foundation, as well as an academic administrator. He is most known in cognitive psychology for the development of the Atkinson–Shiffrin model of memory, which distinguished between short- and long-term memory.

Bernard J. Baars (b. 1946) is a Dutch-born psychologist and Fellow at the Neurosciences Institute in La Jolla, CA. He is best known for his work on the relationship between brain structures and consciousness.

Donald Broadbent (1926–93) was a British experimental psychologist, former director of the Applied Psychology Research Unit at the University of Cambridge, and early advisor to Alan D. Baddeley. He is well known for his work on attention and short-term memory, as well as for his text, *Perception and Communication*, which remains a seminal work in cognitive psychology.

Patricia A. Carpenter is an American psychologist at Carnegie Mellon University. Her work generally examines the structure and organization of the brain while performing cognitive tasks.

R. Conrad was a British psychologist at the Applied Psychology Research Unit at the University of Cambridge and an early advisor to Alan D. Baddeley. He is known for his work on short-term memory and, specifically, the acoustic similarity effect.

Fergus I. M. Craik (b. 1935) is a British cognitive psychologist and was professor at the University of Toronto from 1971 to 2000. He is well known for his research on levels of processing in memory—

essentially that the more depth and meaning are given to information, the more memorable it becomes.

Meredyth Daneman is a cognitive psychologist and professor and department chair at the University of Toronto, Mississauga. She is most known for her work on reading comprehension and individual differences in working memory as a predictor of reading comprehension.

Randall W. Engle is a cognitive psychologist and professor at the Georgia Institute of Technology. He is known for his work on working memory capacity—the amount of information that working memory can process.

Susan Gathercole is a British psychologist and director at the University of Cambridge's Cognition and Brain Sciences Unit. She is most known for her research on working memory deficits in children.

David Z. Hambrick is an American cognitive psychologist and professor at Michigan State University. He is known for his research on working memory and predictors of success and expertise.

John Jonides is an American cognitive psychologist and neuroscientist and professor at the University of Michigan. He is known for his research examining memory with the aid of neuroimaging techniques.

Imre Lakatos (1922–74) was a Hungarian philosopher of math and science. He is known for proposing a structure to theories that gives varying weight to different assumptions. In other words, some assumptions are viewed as needing to be always true to sustain the theory, while other assumptions can have less rigid requirements.

Robert S. Lockhart is a cognitive psychologist and professor at the University of Toronto. He is well known for his research on levels of processing in memory—which essentially found that the more depth and meaning are given to information, the more memorable it becomes.

Robert Logie is a British cognitive psychologist and professor at the University of Edinburgh. He is known for his research on working memory and how it changes and develops over a life-span. He is also a longtime collaborator of Alan Baddeley's.

Karl Popper (1902–94) was an Austrian-British philosopher of science. He is known for his promotion of the importance of falsification in science. That is, while it is difficult to prove theories, it is possible to disprove theories, and therefore scientists should strive for a theory that withstands empirical scrutiny.

Jeroen G. W. Raaijmakers (b. 1952) is a Dutch cognitive psychologist and professor at the University of Amsterdam. He is known for his work on the structure of the entire memory system.

Richard M. Shiffrin (b. 1942) is an American cognitive psychologist and professor at Indiana University, Bloomington. He is known for his extensive research on attention and memory. During the early stage of his career, he also developed the Atkinson–Shiffrin model of memory.

Edward E. Smith (1940–2012) was an American cognitive psychologist. He was known for his research on memory, learning, and in neuroscience.

Tor D. Wager is an American cognitive psychologist and neuroscientist and currently professor at the University of Colorado, Boulder. He is known for his research on how the brain processes pain.

John B. Watson (1878–1958) was an American psychologist and founder of behaviorism. He is known for applying the behaviorist approach to many areas—including child-rearing, animal behavior, and advertising.

WORKS CITED

WORKS CITED

Atkinson, Richard C., and Richard M. Shiffrin. *The Control Processes of Short-term Memory*. Institute for Mathematical Studies in the Social Sciences. Stanford, CA: Stanford University, 1971.

———. "Human Memory: A Proposed System and Its Control Processes," *The Psychology of Learning and Motivation: Advances in Research and Theory*, vol. 2, ed. Kenneth W. Spence and Janet T. Spence (New York: Academic Press, 1968), 89–195.

Baars, Bernard J. *A cognitive theory of consciousness*. Cambridge University Press, 1993.

Baddeley, Alan D. "Alan Baddeley on the Cognitive Revolution." YouTube video, 5:10, posted by "gocognitive," October 27, 2010. https://www.youtube.com/watch?v=wyfEETtWgCY.

———. "Awards for Distinguished Scientific Contributions Is Working Memory Still Working?" *American Psychologist* 56, no. 11 (2001): 849.

———. "The Episodic Buffer: A New Component of Working Memory?" *Trends in Cognitive Sciences* 4, no. 11 (2000): 417–23.

———. "Working memory." *Science* 255, no. 5044 (1992): 556–9.

———. "Working Memory: Theories, Models, and Controversies." *Annual Review of Psychology* 63 (2012): 1–29.

Baddeley, Alan D., and Graham Hitch. "The Recency Effect: Implicit Learning with Explicit Retrieval?" *Memory & Cognition* 21, no. 2 (1993): 146–55.

———. "Working Memory." *Psychology of Learning and Motivation* 8 (1974): 47–89.

Baddeley, Alan, Robert Logie, Ian Nimmo-Smith, and Neil Brereton. "Components of Fluent Reading." *Journal of Memory and Language* 24, no. 1 (1985): 119–31.

Broadbent, Donald E. *Perception and Communication*. Elmsford: Pergamon Press, 1958.

Craik, Fergus I. M., and Robert S. Lockhart. "Levels of Processing: A Framework for Memory Research." *Journal of Verbal Learning and Verbal Behavior* 11 (1972): 671–84.

Daneman, Meredyth, and Patricia A. Carpenter. "Individual Differences in Working Memory and Reading." *Journal of Verbal Learning and Verbal Behavior* 19, no. 4 (1980): 451–66.

Gathercole, Susan E., and Alan D. Baddeley. "Phonological Memory Deficits in Language Disordered Children: Is There a Causal Connection?" *Journal of Memory and Language* 29, no. 3 (1990): 336–60.

Groeger, John. "The Working Memory Man." *The Psychologist* 7, no. 2 (1994): 58–9.

Hambrick, David Z., and Randall W. Engle. "The Role of Working Memory in Problem Solving." *The Psychology of Problem Solving* (2003): 176–206.

"Interview with Alan Baddeley." *The Psychologist*. Accessed June 5, 2015. https://thepsychologist.bps.org.uk/volume-24/edition-5/interview-alan-baddeley

Jonides, John, Richard L. Lewis, Derek Evan Nee, Cindy A. Lustig, Marc G. Berman, and Katherine Sledge Moore. "The Mind and Brain of Short-Term Memory." *Annual Review of Psychology* 59 (2008): 216–24.

"Looking Back: How it All Began." *The Psychologist*. Accessed June 5, 2015. https://thepsychologist.bps.org.uk/volume-28/april-2015/looking-back-how-it-all-began

Miller, George A. "The Magical Number Seven, Plus or Minus Two: Some Limits on Our Capacity for Processing Information." *Psychological Review* 63, no. 2 (1956): 81–97.

Raaijmakers, Jeroen G. W. "The Story of the Two-Store Model of Memory: Past Criticisms, Current Status, and Future Directions," in *Attention and Performance XIV (Silver Jubilee volume)*, ed. David E. Meyer and Sylvan Kornblum (Cambridge, MA: MIT Press, 1993), 467-488.

Shannon, Claude Elwood. "A Mathematical Theory of Communication." *ACM SIGMOBILE Mobile Computing and Communications Review* 5, no. 1 (2001): 3–55.

Smith, Edward E., Stephen Michael Kosslyn, and Lawrence W. Barsalou. *Cognitive Psychology: Mind and Brain*. Upper Saddle River, NJ: Pearson Prentice Hall, 2007.

Wager, Tor D., and Edward E. Smith. "Neuroimaging Studies of Working Memory." *Cognitive, Affective, & Behavioral Neuroscience* 3, no. 4 (2003): 255–74.

Watson, John B. Behaviorism. New York: W. W. Norton & Company, Inc., 1925.

THE MACAT LIBRARY
BY DISCIPLINE

The Macat Library By Discipline

AFRICANA STUDIES

Chinua Achebe's *An Image of Africa: Racism in Conrad's Heart of Darkness*
W. E. B. Du Bois's *The Souls of Black Folk*
Zora Neale Huston's *Characteristics of Negro Expression*
Martin Luther King Jr's *Why We Can't Wait*
Toni Morrison's *Playing in the Dark: Whiteness in the American Literary Imagination*

ANTHROPOLOGY

Arjun Appadurai's *Modernity at Large: Cultural Dimensions of Globalisation*
Philippe Ariès's *Centuries of Childhood*
Franz Boas's *Race, Language and Culture*
Kim Chan & Renée Mauborgne's *Blue Ocean Strategy*
Jared Diamond's *Guns, Germs & Steel: the Fate of Human Societies*
Jared Diamond's *Collapse: How Societies Choose to Fail or Survive*
E. E. Evans-Pritchard's *Witchcraft, Oracles and Magic Among the Azande*
James Ferguson's *The Anti-Politics Machine*
Clifford Geertz's *The Interpretation of Cultures*
David Graeber's *Debt: the First 5000 Years*
Karen Ho's *Liquidated: An Ethnography of Wall Street*
Geert Hofstede's *Culture's Consequences: Comparing Values, Behaviors, Institutes and Organizations across Nations*
Claude Lévi-Strauss's *Structural Anthropology*
Jay Macleod's *Ain't No Makin' It: Aspirations and Attainment in a Low-Income Neighborhood*
Saba Mahmood's *The Politics of Piety: The Islamic Revival and the Feminist Subject*
Marcel Mauss's *The Gift*

BUSINESS

Jean Lave & Etienne Wenger's *Situated Learning*
Theodore Levitt's *Marketing Myopia*
Burton G. Malkiel's *A Random Walk Down Wall Street*
Douglas McGregor's *The Human Side of Enterprise*
Michael Porter's *Competitive Strategy: Creating and Sustaining Superior Performance*
John Kotter's *Leading Change*
C. K. Prahalad & Gary Hamel's *The Core Competence of the Corporation*

CRIMINOLOGY

Michelle Alexander's *The New Jim Crow: Mass Incarceration in the Age of Colorblindness*
Michael R. Gottfredson & Travis Hirschi's *A General Theory of Crime*
Richard Herrnstein & Charles A. Murray's *The Bell Curve: Intelligence and Class Structure in American Life*
Elizabeth Loftus's *Eyewitness Testimony*
Jay Macleod's *Ain't No Makin' It: Aspirations and Attainment in a Low-Income Neighborhood*
Philip Zimbardo's *The Lucifer Effect*

ECONOMICS

Janet Abu-Lughod's *Before European Hegemony*
Ha-Joon Chang's *Kicking Away the Ladder*
David Brion Davis's *The Problem of Slavery in the Age of Revolution*
Milton Friedman's *The Role of Monetary Policy*
Milton Friedman's *Capitalism and Freedom*
David Graeber's *Debt: the First 5000 Years*
Friedrich Hayek's *The Road to Serfdom*
Karen Ho's *Liquidated: An Ethnography of Wall Street*

John Maynard Keynes's *The General Theory of Employment, Interest and Money*
Charles P. Kindleberger's *Manias, Panics and Crashes*
Robert Lucas's *Why Doesn't Capital Flow from Rich to Poor Countries?*
Burton G. Malkiel's *A Random Walk Down Wall Street*
Thomas Robert Malthus's *An Essay on the Principle of Population*
Karl Marx's *Capital*
Thomas Piketty's *Capital in the Twenty-First Century*
Amartya Sen's *Development as Freedom*
Adam Smith's *The Wealth of Nations*
Nassim Nicholas Taleb's *The Black Swan: The Impact of the Highly Improbable*
Amos Tversky's & Daniel Kahneman's *Judgment under Uncertainty: Heuristics and Biases*
Mahbub Ul Haq's *Reflections on Human Development*
Max Weber's *The Protestant Ethic and the Spirit of Capitalism*

FEMINISM AND GENDER STUDIES

Judith Butler's *Gender Trouble*
Simone De Beauvoir's *The Second Sex*
Michel Foucault's *History of Sexuality*
Betty Friedan's *The Feminine Mystique*
Saba Mahmood's *The Politics of Piety: The Islamic Revival and the Feminist Subject*
Joan Wallach Scott's *Gender and the Politics of History*
Mary Wollstonecraft's *A Vindication of the Rights of Woman*
Virginia Woolf's *A Room of One's Own*

GEOGRAPHY

The Brundtland Report's *Our Common Future*
Rachel Carson's *Silent Spring*
Charles Darwin's *On the Origin of Species*
James Ferguson's *The Anti-Politics Machine*
Jane Jacobs's *The Death and Life of Great American Cities*
James Lovelock's *Gaia: A New Look at Life on Earth*
Amartya Sen's *Development as Freedom*
Mathis Wackernagel & William Rees's *Our Ecological Footprint*

HISTORY

Janet Abu-Lughod's *Before European Hegemony*
Benedict Anderson's *Imagined Communities*
Bernard Bailyn's *The Ideological Origins of the American Revolution*
Hanna Batatu's *The Old Social Classes And The Revolutionary Movements Of Iraq*
Christopher Browning's *Ordinary Men: Reserve Police Batallion 101 and the Final Solution in Poland*
Edmund Burke's *Reflections on the Revolution in France*
William Cronon's *Nature's Metropolis: Chicago And The Great West*
Alfred W. Crosby's *The Columbian Exchange*
Hamid Dabashi's *Iran: A People Interrupted*
David Brion Davis's *The Problem of Slavery in the Age of Revolution*
Nathalie Zemon Davis's *The Return of Martin Guerre*
Jared Diamond's *Guns, Germs & Steel: the Fate of Human Societies*
Frank Dikotter's *Mao's Great Famine*
John W Dower's *War Without Mercy: Race And Power In The Pacific War*
W. E. B. Du Bois's *The Souls of Black Folk*
Richard J. Evans's *In Defence of History*
Lucien Febvre's *The Problem of Unbelief in the 16th Century*
Sheila Fitzpatrick's *Everyday Stalinism*

The Macat Library By Discipline

Eric Foner's *Reconstruction: America's Unfinished Revolution, 1863-1877*
Michel Foucault's *Discipline and Punish*
Michel Foucault's *History of Sexuality*
Francis Fukuyama's *The End of History and the Last Man*
John Lewis Gaddis's *We Now Know: Rethinking Cold War History*
Ernest Gellner's *Nations and Nationalism*
Eugene Genovese's *Roll, Jordan, Roll: The World the Slaves Made*
Carlo Ginzburg's *The Night Battles*
Daniel Goldhagen's *Hitler's Willing Executioners*
Jack Goldstone's *Revolution and Rebellion in the Early Modern World*
Antonio Gramsci's *The Prison Notebooks*
Alexander Hamilton, John Jay & James Madison's *The Federalist Papers*
Christopher Hill's *The World Turned Upside Down*
Carole Hillenbrand's *The Crusades: Islamic Perspectives*
Thomas Hobbes's *Leviathan*
Eric Hobsbawm's *The Age Of Revolution*
John A. Hobson's *Imperialism: A Study*
Albert Hourani's *History of the Arab Peoples*
Samuel P. Huntington's *The Clash of Civilizations and the Remaking of World Order*
C. L. R. James's *The Black Jacobins*
Tony Judt's *Postwar: A History of Europe Since 1945*
Ernst Kantorowicz's *The King's Two Bodies: A Study in Medieval Political Theology*
Paul Kennedy's *The Rise and Fall of the Great Powers*
Ian Kershaw's *The "Hitler Myth": Image and Reality in the Third Reich*
John Maynard Keynes's *The General Theory of Employment, Interest and Money*
Charles P. Kindleberger's *Manias, Panics and Crashes*
Martin Luther King Jr's *Why We Can't Wait*
Henry Kissinger's *World Order: Reflections on the Character of Nations and the Course of History*
Thomas Kuhn's *The Structure of Scientific Revolutions*
Georges Lefebvre's *The Coming of the French Revolution*
John Locke's *Two Treatises of Government*
Niccolò Machiavelli's *The Prince*
Thomas Robert Malthus's *An Essay on the Principle of Population*
Mahmood Mamdani's *Citizen and Subject: Contemporary Africa And The Legacy Of Late Colonialism*
Karl Marx's *Capital*
Stanley Milgram's *Obedience to Authority*
John Stuart Mill's *On Liberty*
Thomas Paine's *Common Sense*
Thomas Paine's *Rights of Man*
Geoffrey Parker's *Global Crisis: War, Climate Change and Catastrophe in the Seventeenth Century*
Jonathan Riley-Smith's *The First Crusade and the Idea of Crusading*
Jean-Jacques Rousseau's *The Social Contract*
Joan Wallach Scott's *Gender and the Politics of History*
Theda Skocpol's *States and Social Revolutions*
Adam Smith's *The Wealth of Nations*
Timothy Snyder's *Bloodlands: Europe Between Hitler and Stalin*
Sun Tzu's *The Art of War*
Keith Thomas's *Religion and the Decline of Magic*
Thucydides's *The History of the Peloponnesian War*
Frederick Jackson Turner's *The Significance of the Frontier in American History*
Odd Arne Westad's *The Global Cold War: Third World Interventions And The Making Of Our Times*

LITERATURE

Chinua Achebe's *An Image of Africa: Racism in Conrad's Heart of Darkness*
Roland Barthes's *Mythologies*
Homi K. Bhabha's *The Location of Culture*
Judith Butler's *Gender Trouble*
Simone De Beauvoir's *The Second Sex*
Ferdinand De Saussure's *Course in General Linguistics*
T. S. Eliot's *The Sacred Wood: Essays on Poetry and Criticism*
Zora Neale Huston's *Characteristics of Negro Expression*
Toni Morrison's *Playing in the Dark: Whiteness in the American Literary Imagination*
Edward Said's *Orientalism*
Gayatri Chakravorty Spivak's *Can the Subaltern Speak?*
Mary Wollstonecraft's *A Vindication of the Rights of Women*
Virginia Woolf's *A Room of One's Own*

PHILOSOPHY

Elizabeth Anscombe's *Modern Moral Philosophy*
Hannah Arendt's *The Human Condition*
Aristotle's *Metaphysics*
Aristotle's *Nicomachean Ethics*
Edmund Gettier's *Is Justified True Belief Knowledge?*
Georg Wilhelm Friedrich Hegel's *Phenomenology of Spirit*
David Hume's *Dialogues Concerning Natural Religion*
David Hume's *The Enquiry for Human Understanding*
Immanuel Kant's *Religion within the Boundaries of Mere Reason*
Immanuel Kant's *Critique of Pure Reason*
Søren Kierkegaard's *The Sickness Unto Death*
Søren Kierkegaard's *Fear and Trembling*
C. S. Lewis's *The Abolition of Man*
Alasdair MacIntyre's *After Virtue*
Marcus Aurelius's *Meditations*
Friedrich Nietzsche's *On the Genealogy of Morality*
Friedrich Nietzsche's *Beyond Good and Evil*
Plato's *Republic*
Plato's *Symposium*
Jean-Jacques Rousseau's *The Social Contract*
Gilbert Ryle's *The Concept of Mind*
Baruch Spinoza's *Ethics*
Sun Tzu's *The Art of War*
Ludwig Wittgenstein's *Philosophical Investigations*

POLITICS

Benedict Anderson's *Imagined Communities*
Aristotle's *Politics*
Bernard Bailyn's *The Ideological Origins of the American Revolution*
Edmund Burke's *Reflections on the Revolution in France*
John C. Calhoun's *A Disquisition on Government*
Ha-Joon Chang's *Kicking Away the Ladder*
Hamid Dabashi's *Iran: A People Interrupted*
Hamid Dabashi's *Theology of Discontent: The Ideological Foundation of the Islamic Revolution in Iran*
Robert Dahl's *Democracy and its Critics*
Robert Dahl's *Who Governs?*
David Brion Davis's *The Problem of Slavery in the Age of Revolution*

The Macat Library By Discipline

Alexis De Tocqueville's *Democracy in America*
James Ferguson's *The Anti-Politics Machine*
Frank Dikotter's *Mao's Great Famine*
Sheila Fitzpatrick's *Everyday Stalinism*
Eric Foner's *Reconstruction: America's Unfinished Revolution, 1863-1877*
Milton Friedman's *Capitalism and Freedom*
Francis Fukuyama's *The End of History and the Last Man*
John Lewis Gaddis's *We Now Know: Rethinking Cold War History*
Ernest Gellner's *Nations and Nationalism*
David Graeber's *Debt: the First 5000 Years*
Antonio Gramsci's *The Prison Notebooks*
Alexander Hamilton, John Jay & James Madison's *The Federalist Papers*
Friedrich Hayek's *The Road to Serfdom*
Christopher Hill's *The World Turned Upside Down*
Thomas Hobbes's *Leviathan*
John A. Hobson's *Imperialism: A Study*
Samuel P. Huntington's *The Clash of Civilizations and the Remaking of World Order*
Tony Judt's *Postwar: A History of Europe Since 1945*
David C. Kang's *China Rising: Peace, Power and Order in East Asia*
Paul Kennedy's *The Rise and Fall of Great Powers*
Robert Keohane's *After Hegemony*
Martin Luther King Jr.'s *Why We Can't Wait*
Henry Kissinger's *World Order: Reflections on the Character of Nations and the Course of History*
John Locke's *Two Treatises of Government*
Niccolò Machiavelli's *The Prince*
Thomas Robert Malthus's *An Essay on the Principle of Population*
Mahmood Mamdani's *Citizen and Subject: Contemporary Africa And The Legacy Of Late Colonialism*
Karl Marx's *Capital*
John Stuart Mill's *On Liberty*
John Stuart Mill's *Utilitarianism*
Hans Morgenthau's *Politics Among Nations*
Thomas Paine's *Common Sense*
Thomas Paine's *Rights of Man*
Thomas Piketty's *Capital in the Twenty-First Century*
Robert D. Putman's *Bowling Alone*
John Rawls's *Theory of Justice*
Jean-Jacques Rousseau's *The Social Contract*
Theda Skocpol's *States and Social Revolutions*
Adam Smith's *The Wealth of Nations*
Sun Tzu's *The Art of War*
Henry David Thoreau's *Civil Disobedience*
Thucydides's *The History of the Peloponnesian War*
Kenneth Waltz's *Theory of International Politics*
Max Weber's *Politics as a Vocation*
Odd Arne Westad's *The Global Cold War: Third World Interventions And The Making Of Our Times*

POSTCOLONIAL STUDIES

Roland Barthes's *Mythologies*
Frantz Fanon's *Black Skin, White Masks*
Homi K. Bhabha's *The Location of Culture*
Gustavo Gutiérrez's *A Theology of Liberation*
Edward Said's *Orientalism*
Gayatri Chakravorty Spivak's *Can the Subaltern Speak?*

PSYCHOLOGY

Gordon Allport's *The Nature of Prejudice*
Alan Baddeley & Graham Hitch's *Aggression: A Social Learning Analysis*
Albert Bandura's *Aggression: A Social Learning Analysis*
Leon Festinger's *A Theory of Cognitive Dissonance*
Sigmund Freud's *The Interpretation of Dreams*
Betty Friedan's *The Feminine Mystique*
Michael R. Gottfredson & Travis Hirschi's *A General Theory of Crime*
Eric Hoffer's *The True Believer: Thoughts on the Nature of Mass Movements*
William James's *Principles of Psychology*
Elizabeth Loftus's *Eyewitness Testimony*
A. H. Maslow's *A Theory of Human Motivation*
Stanley Milgram's *Obedience to Authority*
Steven Pinker's *The Better Angels of Our Nature*
Oliver Sacks's *The Man Who Mistook His Wife For a Hat*
Richard Thaler & Cass Sunstein's *Nudge: Improving Decisions About Health, Wealth and Happiness*
Amos Tversky's *Judgment under Uncertainty: Heuristics and Biases*
Philip Zimbardo's *The Lucifer Effect*

SCIENCE

Rachel Carson's *Silent Spring*
William Cronon's *Nature's Metropolis: Chicago And The Great West*
Alfred W. Crosby's *The Columbian Exchange*
Charles Darwin's *On the Origin of Species*
Richard Dawkin's *The Selfish Gene*
Thomas Kuhn's *The Structure of Scientific Revolutions*
Geoffrey Parker's *Global Crisis: War, Climate Change and Catastrophe in the Seventeenth Century*
Mathis Wackernagel & William Rees's *Our Ecological Footprint*

SOCIOLOGY

Michelle Alexander's *The New Jim Crow: Mass Incarceration in the Age of Colorblindness*
Gordon Allport's *The Nature of Prejudice*
Albert Bandura's *Aggression: A Social Learning Analysis*
Hanna Batatu's *The Old Social Classes And The Revolutionary Movements Of Iraq*
Ha-Joon Chang's *Kicking Away the Ladder*
W. E. B. Du Bois's *The Souls of Black Folk*
Émile Durkheim's *On Suicide*
Frantz Fanon's *Black Skin, White Masks*
Frantz Fanon's *The Wretched of the Earth*
Eric Foner's *Reconstruction: America's Unfinished Revolution, 1863-1877*
Eugene Genovese's *Roll, Jordan, Roll: The World the Slaves Made*
Jack Goldstone's *Revolution and Rebellion in the Early Modern World*
Antonio Gramsci's *The Prison Notebooks*
Richard Herrnstein & Charles A Murray's *The Bell Curve: Intelligence and Class Structure in American Life*
Eric Hoffer's *The True Believer: Thoughts on the Nature of Mass Movements*
Jane Jacobs's *The Death and Life of Great American Cities*
Robert Lucas's *Why Doesn't Capital Flow from Rich to Poor Countries?*
Jay Macleod's *Ain't No Makin' It: Aspirations and Attainment in a Low Income Neighborhood*
Elaine May's *Homeward Bound: American Families in the Cold War Era*
Douglas McGregor's *The Human Side of Enterprise*
C. Wright Mills's *The Sociological Imagination*

Thomas Piketty's *Capital in the Twenty-First Century*
Robert D. Putman's *Bowling Alone*
David Riesman's *The Lonely Crowd: A Study of the Changing American Character*
Edward Said's *Orientalism*
Joan Wallach Scott's *Gender and the Politics of History*
Theda Skocpol's *States and Social Revolutions*
Max Weber's *The Protestant Ethic and the Spirit of Capitalism*

THEOLOGY

Augustine's *Confessions*
Benedict's *Rule of St Benedict*
Gustavo Gutiérrez's *A Theology of Liberation*
Carole Hillenbrand's *The Crusades: Islamic Perspectives*
David Hume's *Dialogues Concerning Natural Religion*
Immanuel Kant's *Religion within the Boundaries of Mere Reason*
Ernst Kantorowicz's *The King's Two Bodies: A Study in Medieval Political Theology*
Søren Kierkegaard's *The Sickness Unto Death*
C. S. Lewis's *The Abolition of Man*
Saba Mahmood's *The Politics of Piety: The Islamic Revival and the Feminist Subjec*t
Baruch Spinoza's *Ethics*
Keith Thomas's *Religion and the Decline of Magic*

COMING SOON

Chris Argyris's *The Individual and the Organisation*
Seyla Benhabib's *The Rights of Others*
Walter Benjamin's *The Work Of Art in the Age of Mechanical Reproduction*
John Berger's *Ways of Seeing*
Pierre Bourdieu's *Outline of a Theory of Practice*
Mary Douglas's *Purity and Danger*
Roland Dworkin's *Taking Rights Seriously*
James G. March's *Exploration and Exploitation in Organisational Learning*
Ikujiro Nonaka's *A Dynamic Theory of Organizational Knowledge Creation*
Griselda Pollock's *Vision and Difference*
Amartya Sen's *Inequality Re-Examined*
Susan Sontag's *On Photography*
Yasser Tabbaa's *The Transformation of Islamic Art*
Ludwig von Mises's *Theory of Money and Credit*

Macat Disciplines

Access the greatest ideas and thinkers across entire disciplines, including

FEMINISM, GENDER AND QUEER STUDIES

Simone De Beauvoir's
The Second Sex

Michel Foucault's
History of Sexuality

Betty Friedan's
The Feminine Mystique

Saba Mahmood's
*The Politics of Piety:
The Islamic Revival and
the Feminist Subject*

Joan Wallach Scott's
*Gender and the
Politics of History*

Mary Wollstonecraft's
*A Vindication of the
Rights of Woman*

Virginia Woolf's
A Room of One's Own

Judith Butler's
Gender Trouble

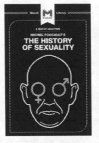

Macat analyses are available from all good bookshops and libraries.

Access hundreds of analyses through one, multimedia tool.
Join free for one month **library.macat.com**

Macat Disciplines

Access the greatest ideas and thinkers across entire disciplines, including

INEQUALITY

Ha-Joon Chang's, *Kicking Away the Ladder*

David Graeber's, *Debt: The First 5000 Years*

Robert E. Lucas's, *Why Doesn't Capital Flow from Rich To Poor Countries?*

Thomas Piketty's, *Capital in the Twenty-First Century*

Amartya Sen's, *Inequality Re-Examined*

Mahbub Ul Haq's, *Reflections on Human Development*

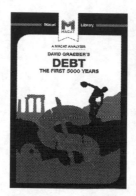

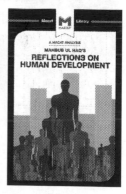

Macat analyses are available from all good bookshops and libraries.

Access hundreds of analyses through one, multimedia tool.
Join free for one month **library.macat.com**

Macat Disciplines

Access the greatest ideas and thinkers
across entire disciplines, including

CRIMINOLOGY

Michelle Alexander's
The New Jim Crow:
Mass Incarceration in the
Age of Colorblindness

Michael R. Gottfredson
& Travis Hirschi's
A General Theory of Crime

Elizabeth Loftus's
Eyewitness Testimony

Richard Herrnstein
& Charles A. Murray's
The Bell Curve: Intelligence and
Class Structure in American Life

Jay Macleod's
Ain't No Makin' It:
Aspirations and Attainment in a
Low-Income Neighborhood

Philip Zimbardo's
The Lucifer Effect

Macat analyses are available from all good bookshops and libraries.

Access hundreds of analyses through one, multimedia tool.
Join free for one month **library.macat.com**

Macat Disciplines

Access the greatest ideas and thinkers across entire disciplines, including

Postcolonial Studies

Roland Barthes's *Mythologies*
Frantz Fanon's *Black Skin, White Masks*
Homi K. Bhabha's *The Location of Culture*
Gustavo Gutiérrez's *A Theology of Liberation*
Edward Said's *Orientalism*
Gayatri Chakravorty Spivak's *Can the Subaltern Speak?*

Macat analyses are available from all good bookshops and libraries.

Access hundreds of analyses through one, multimedia tool.
Join free for one month **library.macat.com**

Printed in the United States
by Baker & Taylor Publisher Services